English Language, Literature, and Composition
Content Knowledge
Study Guide

▶ ▶ ▶ ▶ ▶ ▶ ▶ ▶ ▶ ▶ ▶ ▶

A PUBLICATION OF EDUCATIONAL TESTING SERVICE

Table of Contents
Study Guide for the *English Language, Literature, and Composition: Content Knowledge* Test

▶   ▶   ▶   ▶   ▶   ▶   ▶   ▶   ▶   ▶   ▶   ▶

TABLE OF CONTENTS

Chapter 1
Introduction to *English Language, Literature, and Composition: Content Knowledge* and Suggestions for Using this Study Guide

►   ►   ►   ►   ►   ►   ►   ►   ►   ►   ►   ►

Introduction to *English Language, Literature, and Composition: Content Knowledge*

The *English Language, Literature, and Composition: Content Knowledge* test is designed for prospective secondary English teachers. The test is designed to reflect current standards for knowledge, skills, and abilities in language arts education. Educational Testing Service (ETS) works in collaboration with the National Council of Teachers of English (NCTE) and the National Council for Accreditation of Teacher Education (NCATE), along with teacher educators, higher education content specialists, and accomplished practicing teachers in the field of language arts to keep the test updated and representative of current standards.

The test consists of 120 multiple-choice questions and covers three major areas, in the following proportions:

- Reading and Understanding Text (55%)

- Language and Linguistics (15%)

- Composition and Rhetoric (30%)

Test takers have two hours to complete the test.

The test is not intended to assess teaching skills but rather to demonstrate the candidate's fundamental knowledge in the major areas of the language arts.

Suggestions for Using the "Study Topics" Chapter

This test is different from a final exam or other tests you may have taken in that it is comprehensive — that is, it covers material you may have learned in several courses during more than one year. It requires you to synthesize information you have learned from many sources and to understand the subject as a whole.

As a teacher, you will need a thorough understanding of the fundamental concepts of the field and the ways in which the various concepts fit together. You also need to understand typical misconceptions, because as a teacher you will need to apply your knowledge to situations in the classroom.

This test is very different from the SAT® or other assessments of your reading, writing, and mathematical skills. You may have heard it said that you can't study for the SAT — that is, you should have learned these skills throughout your school years, and you can't learn reading or reasoning skills shortly before you take the exam. The *English Language, Literature, and Composition: Content Knowledge* test assesses a domain you *can* review for and *can* prepare to be tested on. Moreover, studying for your licensing exam is a great opportunity to reflect on your field and develop a deeper understanding of it before you begin to teach the subject matter to others.

We recommend the following approach for using the "Study Topics" chapter to prepare for the test.

Become familiar with the test content. Learn what will be assessed in the test, covered in chapter 3.

Assess how well you know the content in each area. It is quite likely that you will need to study in most or all of the areas. After you learn what the test contains, you should assess your knowledge in each area. How well do you know the material? In which areas do you need to learn more before you take the test?

Develop a study plan. Assess what you need to study and create a realistic plan for studying. You can develop your study plan in any way that works best for you. A "Study Plan" form is included in Appendix A at the end of the book as a possible way to structure your planning. Remember that this is a licensure test and covers a great deal of material. Plan to review carefully. You will need to allow time to find the books and other materials, time to read the material and take notes, and time to go over your notes.

Identify study materials. Most of the material covered by the test is contained in standard introductory textbooks. If you do not own introductory texts that cover all the areas, you may want to borrow one or more from friends or from a library. You may also want to obtain a copy of your state's standards for language arts. (One way to find these standards quickly is to go to the Web site for your state's Department of Education.) The textbooks used in secondary classrooms may also prove useful to you, since they also present the material you need to know. Use standard school and college introductory textbooks and other reliable, professionally prepared materials. Don't rely heavily on information provided by friends or from searching the World Wide Web. Neither of these sources is as uniformly reliable as textbooks.

Work through your study plan. You may want to work alone, or you may find it more helpful to work with a group or with a mentor. Work through the topics and questions provided in chapter 3. Be able to define and discuss the topics in your own words rather than memorizing definitions from books. If you are working with a group or mentor, you can also try informal quizzes and questioning techniques.

Proceed to the practice questions. Once you have completed your review, you are ready to benefit from the "Practice Questions" portion of this guide.

Suggestions for using the "Practice Questions" and "Right Answers and Explanations for the Practice Questions" chapters

Read chapter 4. This chapter will sharpen your skills in reading and answering questions. Succeeding on multiple-choice questions requires careful focus on the question, an eye for detail, and patient sifting of the answer choices.

Answer the practice questions in chapter 5. Make your own test-taking conditions as similar to actual testing conditions as you can. Work on the practice questions in a quiet place without distractions. Remember that the practice questions are only examples of the way the topics are covered in the test. The test you take will have different questions.

Score the practice questions. Go through the detailed answers in chapter 6 and mark the questions you answered correctly and the ones you missed. Look over the explanations of the questions you missed and see if you understand them.

Decide whether you need more review. After you have looked at your results, decide if there are areas that you need to brush up on before taking the actual test. (The practice questions are grouped by topic, which may help you to spot areas of particular strength or weakness.) Go back to your textbooks and reference materials to see if the topics are covered there. You might also want to go over your questions with a friend or teacher who is familiar with the subjects.

Assess your readiness. Do you feel confident about your level of understanding in each of the areas? If not, where do you need more work? If you feel ready, complete the checklist in chapter 7 to double-check that you've thought through the details. If you need more information about registration or the testing situation itself, use the resources in Appendix B.

Chapter 2
Background Information on The Praxis Series™ Assessments

▶ ▶ ▶ ▶ ▶ ▶ ▶ ▶ ▶ ▶ ▶ ▶

What are The Praxis Series Subject Assessments?

The Praxis Series Subject Assessments are designed by Educational Testing Service (ETS) to assess your knowledge of the subject area you plan to teach, and they are a part of the licensing procedure in many states. This study guide covers an assessment that tests your knowledge of the actual content you hope to be licensed to teach. Your state has adopted The Praxis Series tests because it wants to be certain that you have achieved a specified level of mastery of your subject area before it grants you a license to teach in a classroom.

The Praxis Series tests are part of a national testing program, meaning that the test covered in this study guide is used in more than one state. The advantage of taking Praxis tests is that if you want to move to another state that uses The Praxis Series tests, you can transfer your scores to that state. Passing scores are set by states, however, so if you are planning to apply for licensure in another state, you may find that passing scores are different. You can find passing scores for all states that use The Praxis Series tests in the *Understanding Your Praxis Scores* pamphlet, available either in your college's School of Education or by calling (609) 771-7395.

What is Licensure?

Licensure in any area — medicine, law, architecture, accounting, cosmetology — is an assurance to the public that the person holding the license has demonstrated a certain level of competence. The phrase used in licensure is that the person holding the license *will do no harm*. In the case of teacher licensing, a license tells the public that the person holding the license can be trusted to educate children competently and professionally.

Because a license makes such a serious claim about its holder, licensure tests are usually quite demanding. In some fields licensure tests have more than one part and last for more than one day. Candidates for licensure in all fields plan intensive study as part of their professional preparation: some join study groups, others study alone. But preparing to take a licensure test is, in all cases, a professional activity. Because it assesses your entire body of knowledge or skill for the field you want to enter, preparing for a licensure exam takes planning, discipline, and sustained effort. Studying thoroughly is highly recommended.

Why does My State Require The Praxis Series Assessments?

Your state chose The Praxis Series Assessments because the tests assess the breadth and depth of content — called the "domain" of the test — that your state wants its teachers to possess before they begin to teach. The level of content knowledge, reflected in the passing score, is based on recommendations of panels of teachers and teacher educators in each subject area in each state. The state licensing agency and, in some states, the state legislature ratify the passing scores that have been recommended by panels of teachers.

You can find out the passing score required for The Praxis Series Assessments in your state by looking in the pamphlet *Understanding Your Praxis Scores,* which is free from ETS (see above). If you look through this pamphlet, you will see that not all states use the same test modules, and even when they do, the passing scores can differ from state to state.

What kinds of Tests are The Praxis Series Subject Assessments?

Two kinds of tests comprise The Praxis Series Subject Assessments: multiple choice (for which you select your answer from a list of choices) and constructed response (for which you write a response of your own). Multiple-choice tests can survey a wider domain because they can ask more questions in a limited period of time. Constructed-response tests have far fewer questions, but the questions require you to demonstrate the depth of your knowledge in the area covered.

What do the Tests Measure?

The Praxis Series Subject Assessments are tests of content knowledge. They measure your understanding of the subject area you want to teach. The multiple-choice tests measure a broad range of knowledge across your content area. The constructed-response tests measure your ability to explain in depth a few essential topics in your subject area. The content-specific pedagogy tests, most of which are constructed-response, measure your understanding of how to teach certain fundamental concepts in your field. The tests do not measure your actual teaching ability, however. They measure your knowledge of your subject and of how to teach it. The teachers in your field who help us design and write these tests, and the states that require these tests, do so in the belief that knowledge of subject area is the first requirement for licensing. Your teaching ability is a skill that is measured in other ways: observation, videotaped teaching, or portfolios are typically used by states to measure teaching ability. Teaching combines many complex skills, only some of which can be measured by a single test. The Praxis Series Subject Assessments are designed to measure how thoroughly you understand the material in the subject areas in which you want to be licensed to teach.

How were These Tests Developed?

ETS began the development of The Praxis Series Subject Assessments with a survey. For each subject, teachers around the country in various teaching situations were asked to judge which knowledge and skills a beginning teacher in that subject needs to possess. Professors in schools of education who prepare teachers were asked the same questions. These responses were ranked in order of importance and sent out to hundreds of teachers for review. All of the responses to these surveys (called "job analysis surveys") were analyzed to summarize the judgments of these professionals. From their consensus, we developed the specifications for the multiple-choice and constructed-response tests. Each subject area had a committee of practicing teachers and teacher educators who wrote these specifications (guidelines).

The specifications were reviewed and eventually approved by teachers. From the test specifications, groups of teachers and professional test developers created test questions.

When your state adopted The Praxis Series Subject Assessments, local panels of practicing teachers and teacher educators in each subject area met to examine the tests question by question and evaluate each question for its relevance to beginning teachers in your state. This is called a "validity study." A test is considered "valid" for a job if it measures what people must know and be able to do on that job. For the test to be adopted in your state, teachers in your state must judge that it is valid.

These teachers and teacher educators also performed a "standard-setting study"; that is, they went through the tests question by question and decided, through a rigorous process, how many questions a beginning teacher would be able to answer correctly. From this study emerged a recommended passing score. The final passing score was approved by your state's licensing agency.

In other words, throughout the development process, practitioners in the teaching field — teachers and teacher educators — have determined what the tests would contain. The practitioners in your state determined which tests would be used for licensure in your subject area and helped decide what score would be needed to achieve licensure. This is how professional licensure works in most fields: those who are already licensed oversee the licensing of new practitioners. When you pass The Praxis Series Subject Assessments, you and the practitioners in your state can be assured that you have the knowledge required to begin practicing your profession.

Chapter 3
Study Topics

▶ ▶ ▶ ▶ ▶ ▶ ▶ ▶ ▶ ▶ ▶ ▶

Here is an overview of the areas assessed in the *English Language, Literature, and Composition: Content Knowledge* test:

Reading and Understanding Text
(55% of the questions)

- Paraphrasing and interpreting various types of texts
- Identifying and interpreting figurative language and other literary elements
- Identifying patterns, structures, and characteristics of literary forms and genres
- Situating and interpreting texts within their historical and cultural contexts
- Identifying major works and authors of American, British, and World literature
- Recognizing and identifying various instructional approaches to and elements of teaching reading and textual interpretation

Language and Linguistics
(15% of the questions)

- Understanding the principles of language acquisition and development
- Understanding elements of the history and development of the English language
- Understanding and applying the elements of traditional grammar
- Understanding the elements of semantics

Composition and Rhetoric
(30% of the questions)

- Understanding and applying elements of teaching writing
- Understanding and evaluating rhetorical features in writing

Using the Topic Lists That Follow

You are not expected to be an expert on all aspects of the topics that follow. But you should understand the major characteristics or aspects of each topic and be able to recognize them in various kinds of examples or selections.

Here, for instance, is one of the topic lists in "Understanding and applying elements of teaching writing" under "Composition and Rhetoric":

▶ Some questions will ask what the different tools and response strategies for assessing student writing are and when they may most appropriately be used. Some relevant tools and response strategies include

- Peer review

- Portfolios

- Holistic scoring

- Scoring rubrics

- Self-assessment

- Conferencing

Referring to textbooks, state standards documents, or other sources as needed, make sure you can describe in your own words what each of these tools or strategies is and in what situations it is most appropriate. For example, you should be able to say to yourself, "For holistic scoring, a set of evaluative criteria is used to assess the quality or overall effectiveness of a piece of student work, with a single score or grade given for the complete performance rather than separate scores or grades for separate elements. Holistic scoring is best used when all the elements being assessed are closely related, such as in a persuasive or analytical essay." If you can familiarize yourself with the topics to the point where you can put explanations and definitions into your own words, you will have positioned yourself well for applying these concepts and answering many of the questions on the test.

Special Topics, Questions, and Annotated Passages Marked with Stars

Interspersed throughout the topic list are topics, questions, and annotated passages that are preceded by stars (★) and outlined in boxes. These additions to the topic list show how you might pay attention to particular concepts in preparing for the test. The questions and topics are intended to guide you into more in-depth preparation in certain areas, while the annotated passages are intended to help you check your understanding and interpretation of representative passages of literature. If you study these questions, topics, and annotated passages, you should gain increased understanding of and facility with important subject matter covered on the test. You might want to discuss these with a teacher or mentor.

Reading and Understanding Text

This part of the test emphasizes comprehension, interpretation, and analysis of literary works. Some specific factual knowledge is required, but for most questions, no previous experience with the supplied passages is required (although it is assumed that you have read widely and perceptively in poetry, drama, fiction, and nonfiction from American, British, and World literature). You will need to draw not only on your ability to analyze the elements of a literary passage and to respond to nuances of meaning, tone, imagery, and style, but also on your ability to interpret metaphors, recognize rhetorical and stylistic devices, perceive relationships between parts and wholes, and grasp a speaker's or author's attitude. You will need knowledge of the means by which literary effects are achieved and familiarity with the basic terminology used to discuss literary texts.

Paraphrasing and interpreting (literally and inferentially) various types of texts, including fiction, poetry, essays, and other nonfiction

▶ Some of the questions will ask about a particular word or phrase.

- "In the poem, the phrase 'the menace' refers to..."

- "The poet's use of the word 'sleep' emphasizes which of the following themes?"

- "The comparison of the narrator's memories of his mother to 'diamonds' is particularly appropriate in the context of the excerpt because it ...."

➤ Some of the questions will address the overall passage rather than a single word or phrase.

- "Which of the following best describes the overall theme of the passage?"

- "The author asserts that life is meaningful only if ...."

- "The author's telling of her childhood memories can best be described as..."

- "The author's primary purpose is to..."

Identifying and interpreting figurative language and other literary elements

➤ The questions will test your ability to interpret and analyze such elements as

- Alliteration
- Allusion
- Analogy
- Characterization (through a character's words, thoughts, actions, etc.)
- Cliché
- Dialect or slang
- Diction
- Figurative language (e.g., metaphor, simile, hyperbole, personification)
- Foreshadowing
- Imagery

- Irony
- Mood
- Point of view (e.g., first-person, third-person objective, third-person omniscient)
- Setting (established through description of scenes, colors, smells, etc.)
- Style
- Symbolism
- Tone
- Voice

Identifying patterns, structures, and characteristics of literary forms and genres

➤ Some questions will ask you to recognize the form of a poem or poetic excerpt or to recognize the definition of a poetic form. The primary poetic forms covered on the test include

- Sonnet
- Haiku
- Epic
- Free verse
- Couplet
- Elegy
- Limerick

➤ Some questions may ask you to interpret meters and rhyme schemes in a poem. You will need to analyze patterns and either connect them with a traditional scheme or determine an unconventional use or effect achieved through meter or rhyme.

Some questions may ask you to recognize the definition of a fiction genre or to make comparisons or distinctions among two or more genres. The primary fiction genres covered on the test include

- Novel
- Short story
- Science fiction
- Fable
- Myth
- Legend
- Folk tale
- Fairy tale
- Frame tale
- Mystery
- Historical fiction

Situating and interpreting texts within their historical and cultural contexts

Some questions will ask you to apply your knowledge of various schools of writers and associate the characteristics of their works with the names of writers in the school, the period in which they worked, and/or the titles of important representative works. The schools covered on the test include, but are not limited to,

- Harlem Renaissance (Zora Neale Hurston, Langston Hughes, Countee Cullen)

- British Romantics (John Keats, Percy Bysshe Shelley, Lord Byron)

- Metaphysical poets (John Donne, Andrew Marvell, George Herbert)

- Transcendentalism (Ralph Waldo Emerson, Henry David Thoreau)

Some questions will ask you to use your knowledge of literary history and styles to connect a particular work with the literary era in which it was written, to link stylistic elements in an excerpt with a particular time period or literary movement or to associate a work with a particular historical event, for example:

- "The style of the excerpt is most closely associated with which of the following literary movements?"

- "Which of the following lists correctly presents the works in order of publication, from earliest to latest?"

- "Which of the following is NOT characteristic of the works of the British Romantic poets?"

- "All of the following were written in the eighteenth century EXCEPT ...."

Identifying major works and authors of American, British, and World literature from various cultures, genres, and periods, including literature for young adults

Some of these questions will ask you to connect a specific author with one of his or her important works. Some questions may ask you to associate specific characters or plot elements with a well-known author or work. You may also be asked to identify an author based on a more general description of the characteristics of that author's works. The following authors are *representative* of those you may be asked to identify.

- Maya Angelou
- Jane Austen
- Ray Bradbury
- Willa Cather
- Stephen Crane
- Emily Dickinson
- Ralph Waldo Emerson
- F. Scott Fitzgerald
- Anne Frank
- Robert Frost
- Zora Neale Hurston
- John Keats
- Harper Lee
- C. S. Lewis
- Herman Melville
- George Orwell
- Edgar Allan Poe
- J. D. Salinger
- William Shakespeare
- Mary Shelley
- Percy Bysshe Shelley
- Amy Tan
- J.R.R. Tolkein
- Mark Twain
- Alice Walker
- Walt Whitman

Exercises related to the "Reading and Understanding Text" topics

The following exercises and annotated samples are intended to give you practice in the kinds of interpretive and analytical thinking about literature that are expected in the "Reading and Understanding Text" section of the test described above. Although the format of these annotation exercises is not like the multiple-choice questions on the test, the types and levels of understanding and evaluation needed to complete them is comparable. For each of the three exercises, read the passage and the questions and try to annotate the passages in response to the questions. Then, for each, read the annotated version on the following page and compare your analysis.

★ Read the following fiction selection, from Ellen Glasgow's story "The Professional Instinct." Describe in your own words the characteristics of Dr. Estbridge. How does the author build this characterization? Why does the author compare Dr. Estbridge's career with a tree? What happens in terms of the narrative in the two sentences beginning with "Long ago..."?

As he unfolded his napkin and broke his toast with the precise touch of fingers that think, Doctor John Estbridge concluded that holidays were becoming unbearable. Christmas again, he reflected gloomily, and Christmas in New York, with a heavy snowstorm that meant weeks of dirt and slush and back-breaking epidemics of influenza and pneumonia! Beyond the curtains of rose-colored damask the storm locked the boughs of an ailanthus tree which grew midway out of the high-fenced backyard. Long ago, in the days of his youth and mania for reform, Estbridge remembered that he had once tried to convert the backyard into an Italian garden. For a brief season box had survived, if it had not actually flourished there, and a cypress tree, sent by an ex-patient from Northern Italy, had lived through a single summer and had died with the first frost of winter. That was nearly twenty years ago, for Estbridge had relinquished his garden with the other dreams of his youth, and to-day the brawny ailanthus stood there as a symbol of the prosperous failure of his career.

★ Here is the same paragraph with annotations that relate to the questions asked on the previous page.

A metaphor vividly depicts the doctor's manual dexterity.

As he unfolded his napkin and broke his toast with the precise touch of fingers that think, Doctor John Estbridge concluded that holidays were becoming unbearable. Christmas again, he reflected gloomily, and Christmas in New York, with a heavy snowstorm that meant weeks of dirt and slush and back-breaking epidemics of influenza and pneumonia! Beyond the curtains of rose-colored damask the storm locked the boughs of an ailanthus tree which grew midway out of the high-fenced backyard. Long ago, in the days of his youth and mania for reform, Estbridge remembered that he had once tried to convert the backyard into an Italian garden. For a brief season box had survived, if it had not actually flourished there, and a cypress tree, sent by an ex-patient from Northern Italy, had lived through a single summer and had died with the first frost of winter. That was nearly twenty years ago, for Estbridge had relinquished his garden with the other dreams of his youth, and to-day the brawny ailanthus stood there as a symbol of the prosperous failure of his career.

In these sentences, Estbridge is not described directly, but through his attitudes toward the holiday and the storm.

The narrative turns to the past, and a significant memory further characterizes Estbridge.

A major theme of the story is that Estbridge is materially successful, but has not led the life he truly wanted to live.

The ailanthus tree gripped in the snow becomes a symbol of Estbridge's career — apparently substantial ("brawny") but nothing like the fulfilling, romantic garden of his dreams.

An oxymoron captures the essence of the characterization.

★ Read the following excerpt from Ted Hughes's poem "The Badlands." What images and techniques does the poet use to depict the landscape of the Badlands National Park? Where does he shift from describing the landscape to describing the sun? What technique is used to depict the sun? Is word repetition important? If so, how? Is there a traditional rhyme scheme? If not, what patterns of sounds are apparent to you?

In the Badlands

We got deeper. A landscape

Staked out in the sun and left to die.

The Theodore Roosevelt National Park.

Long ago dead of the sun. Loose teeth, bone

Coming through crust, bristles.

Or a smashed industrial complex

For production

Of perpetual sacrifice, of canyons

Long ago disemboweled.

When Aztec and Inca went on South

They left the sun waiting,

Starved for worship, raging for attention,

Now gone sullenly mad.

As it sank it stared at our car.

Middle distance, yellow, the Missouri

Crawled, stagnated, crawled.

★ Here is the same excerpt with annotations that relate to the questions asked on the previous page.

In the Badlands

The landscape of the park is depicted as dead from violent exposure to the sun.

We got deeper. A landscape

Staked out in the sun and left to die.

The Theodore Roosevelt National Park.

The description of the landscape is intensified because it precedes the name of the actual location — it is as if the poet rushes to present the dramatic description, then remembers to give the name.

Long ago dead of the sun. Loose teeth, bone

Coming through crust, bristles.

The poet uses body elements to evoke the desiccated, crumbling landscape.

The poet uses modern industrial images to describe the barren landscape.

Or a smashed industrial complex

For production

Of perpetual sacrifice, of canyons

Long ago disemboweled.

The hard initial c's and the soft internal s's predominate in these lines and resonate in other lines.

When Aztec and Inca went on South

They left the sun waiting,

Starved for worship, raging for attention,

Now gone sullenly mad.

As it sank it stared at our car.

The focus shifts from the landscape to the sun. The poet personifies the sun as a god/person, abandoned by its former worshippers, who remains behind, fierce and demented.

The poet turns to the sluggish movement of the Missouri river, using three verbs, "Crawled, stagnated, crawled." The repetition of "crawled" hints that the alternation in the river's movement is endlessly repeated.

Middle distance, yellow, the Missouri

Crawled, stagnated, crawled.

The four images — the decaying body in the desert, the "smashed industrial complex," the angry, ruthless, abandoned sun, and the stagnating and crawling river — together create intense feelings of pain and alienation.

★ A "great picture" painted by Pieter Brueghel in the sixteenth century inspired the following poem, "The Dance," by William Carlos Williams. The painting shows a colorful, boisterous dance at a wedding feast (or "Kermess"). Williams responds to the painting, which is, of course, silent, in a twelve-line poem emphasizing sounds, rhythms, and energetic dance-patterns.

Read the poem. What sounds are repeated? What metrical or rhythmic techniques are used? What other structural or literary techniques are used?

In Brueghel's great picture, *The Kermess*,

the dancers go round, they go round and

around, the squeal and the blare and the

tweedle of bagpipes, a bugle and fiddles

tipping their bellies (round as the thick-

sided glasses whose wash they impound)

their hips and their bellies off balance

to turn them. Kicking and rolling about

the Fair Grounds, swinging their butts, those

shanks must be sound to bear up under such

rollicking measures, prance as they dance

in Bruegel's great picture, *The Kermess*.

There is a kinesthetic effect in that the language is immediately dizzying, like the dance itself, and the word "around" at the start of line 3 provides a kind of jolt.

Onomatopoeia is evident in these lines: "squeal," "blare," and "tweedle" evoke the sounds of "bagpipes, a bugle and fiddles."

There is a more refined repetition of sounds here ("prance"/"dance"), suggesting some grace after all of the "rollicking" dances.

★ Here is the same poem with annotations that relate to the questions asked on the previous page.

In Brueghel's great picture, *The Kermess*,

the dancers go round, they go round and

around, the squeal and the blare and the

tweedle of bagpipes, a bugle and fiddles

tipping their bellies (round as the thick-

sided glasses whose wash they impound)

their hips and their bellies off balance

to turn them. Kicking and rolling about

the Fair Grounds, swinging their butts, those

shanks must be sound to bear up under such

rollicking measures, prance as they dance

in Bruegel's great picture, *The Kermess*.

The poem is unrhymed, but some sounds are repeated insistently: "round" appears three times, but the poem also includes the words "around," "impound," and "sound" (with an unexpected meaning — "sturdy" or "solid" — in line 10).

The last line repeats the first line, completing the "round" of the poem.

The anapestic rhythms are dance-like. ($\cup\cup'\cup\cup'\cup\cup'\cup\cup'$). These rhythms evoke the hopping dance of the peasants with their bulging bellies.

Recognizing and identifying various instructional approaches to and elements of teaching reading and textual interpretation

▶ Questions will address basic strategies for reading development in the secondary school, with a focus on the characteristics and purposes of different approaches rather than on pedagogical applications in specific classroom situations.

- Fostering reading appreciation
  - Use of nonprint materials in addition to the assigned text
  - Use of a variety of print materials, including trade books, electronic books, and Internet resources

- Strengthening vocabulary
  - Structural cues: prefixes, roots, and suffixes
  - Context cues: words and phrases around the unknown word
  - Building relationships between words and the concepts they represent

---

★ What are some instructional strategies for each of the following?

- Increasing students' knowledge of prefixes, roots, and suffixes
- Increasing students' ability to use context cues
- Increasing students' command of the relationships between the concepts and the vocabulary used to represent the concepts introduced in their courses

---

- Strengthening comprehension
  - Building students' ability to
    - Identify key concepts
    - Paraphrase key ideas
    - Make predictions
    - Use recognition of text structure or patterns to aid comprehension
    - Choose correct reading strategies
  - Purposes of
    - Skimming
    - Scanning
    - Note taking
    - Concept mapping and other graphic organizers
    - Semantic feature analysis
    - Anticipation guides
  - Instructional techniques to aid comprehension
    - Modeling, including the teacher reading aloud, the teacher demonstrating appropriate responses to new types of challenging questions, and reciprocal teaching
    - Questioning, including questions to reinforce concepts and elicit analysis, synthesis, or evaluation
    - Scaffolding; that is, helping students achieve independence in reading by first giving support and then gradually taking it away as students are ready to do the tasks on their own
    - Activating prior knowledge, including the use of anticipation guides, semantic feature analysis, pretests, and discussions

— Building metacognition, that is, making students aware of reading strategies and how to use those strategies to learn with text; helping students activate self-knowledge and self-monitoring

Language and Linguistics

Understanding the principles of language acquisition and development, including social, cultural, and historical influences and the role and nature of dialects

▶ These questions will address basic knowledge of how language skills develop, and influences on individuals' use of language.

- Dialects, including historical, geographic, and social variations in the use of the English language

- Relationships between pronunciation and spelling, especially in the context of students' misspellings that result from pronunciation

★ What are homophones, and why is it important for students to be aware of them?

- Phases of language development, especially for secondary students learning English

- Strategies for building English proficiency for students with limited English proficiency

★ What are the characteristics of a secondary student new to the United States who is learning English and who is said to have "beginning proficiency" in English? "Intermediate proficiency"? "Advanced proficiency"?

★ For each of the following techniques, think about why it would help students with limited English proficiency in the classroom and think about how it might be successfully implemented in the secondary English/ Language Arts classroom.

- Encouraging socialization in the learning process
- Making content and plans for activities clear and comprehensible rather than relying on various nonverbal cues or understandings
- Teaching study skills along with content material
- One-on-one tutoring
- Adapting assignments to learners' abilities

- Ways in which new learners of English may use syntax and other elements of their first language when they speak or write in English (e.g., differences in vowel sounds, consonant patterns, or syntax)

Understanding elements of the history and development of the English language and American English

- Some questions will test your understanding of the basic history of the English language.

  - The languages from which English is derived

  - The other modern languages to which English is related, and how they are related

  - The general chronology and stages of the development of English, e.g., what is Middle English and when was it used?

- Some questions will test your understanding of how language (morphological, phonological, and semantic aspects) can change over time (e.g., how the meaning of a word can change over time and how certain words can come to be used as different parts of speech, e.g., a noun comes to be used as a verb).

- Some questions will test your understanding of word etymologies—what an etymology is and what kinds of information it can offer.

- Some questions will test your ability to recognize cognates, prefixes, suffixes, or roots.

Understanding and applying the elements of traditional grammar

- Some questions may ask you to identify the grammatical elements in a given sentence or excerpt.

- Other questions may ask you to recognize definitions of various grammatical elements.

- Other questions may present sentences with grammatical errors and ask you to choose the appropriate corrections or identify the kind of error.

- Elements of grammar that may be tested include

  - Parts of speech
    - Noun: proper, common, collective
    - Pronoun
    - Verb
    - Adjective
    - Adverb
    - Preposition
    - Conjunction
    - Phrase
      — Participial phrase
      — Prepositional phrase
      — Appositive phrase
    - Clause
      — Independent clause
      — Dependent clause

  - Syntactical systems
    - Subject-verb agreement
    - Verb tenses: Present, past, present perfect, past perfect, future, and future perfect
    - Voice of verb: active or passive
    - Pronoun-antecedent agreement and weak reference
    - Correct use of infinitive and participle

  - Sentence types
    - Declarative
    - Interrogative
    - Exclamatory
    - Imperative

- Sentence structure
  - Simple
  - Compound
  - Complex
  - Compound-complex
  - Sentence fragment

Understanding the elements of semantics and how these elements affect meaning

▶ Some questions will ask you to recognize how meaning is affected by punctuation or word order.

▶ Some questions will ask you to recognize how words can connote different things based on context.

▶ Some questions will ask you to recognize how euphemism and other semantic strategies are used to obscure or alter meaning.

▶ Some questions will ask you to recognize the role of jargon and how specific disciplines or professions often develop specialized vocabularies for different purposes.

Composition and Rhetoric

Understanding and applying elements of teaching writing

▶ Some questions will test your knowledge of the stages of the writing process (e.g., prewriting, drafting, revising, editing, publishing, and evaluating).

- Appropriate activities at each stage

- How these stages work recursively and/or not necessarily in a prescribed order

▶ You may be given a set of student responses and be asked questions such as
  - "Which of the following wording additions would improve the clarity of sentence 4 ?"
  - "Which student shows the weakest mastery of spelling, punctuation, and syntax?"
  - "Which student needs a strategy for picking a single line of argument and developing it?"
  - "If a student makes several errors like the one in sentence 4, the teacher should plan more instruction or recommend more practice in ..."

▶ Some questions will ask what the different tools and response strategies for assessing student writing are and when they may most appropriately be used. Some relevant and response strategies covered include

- Peer review

- Portfolios

- Holistic scoring

- Scoring rubrics

- Self-assessment

- Conferencing

▶ Some questions will test your knowledge of common research and documentation techniques.

- Gathering and evaluating data using electronic and print media — you may be asked to recognize various sources for gathering information or to recognize criteria for evaluating usefulness of certain kinds of source materials for given research purposes.

- Types of source materials include
  - Reference works (dictionary, encyclopedia, atlas, almanac)
  - Internet (keyword search, databases, bulletin boards)
  - Other sources (books, newspapers and magazines, government publications, professional journals, *Reader's Guide to Periodical Literature*, and primary sources, including reproductions of original documents)
  - Questionnaires, experiences, field studies, and other sources created by the student
- Criteria for evaluating source information include
  - Motives, credibility, and perspectives of the author
  - Date
  - Rigor of the logic
  - Freedom from strong bias, prejudice, and stereotypes
  - Comprehensiveness of the evidence

▶ Some questions will test your ability to read and interpret bibliographical citations, including

- MLA citations

- APA citations

Understanding and evaluating rhetorical features in writing

Passages for these questions will come from a variety of texts, including speeches, essays, literary criticism, editorials, news articles, advertisements, and nonfiction books.

▶ Some questions will test your ability to evaluate, for a given passage, issues of audience and purpose, for example:

- "Which of the following is the most likely intended audience for the passage?"

- "Which of the following is the purpose for which the passage was written?"

- "Which of the following strategies is used in the passage to persuade the reader?"

▶ Some questions will test your ability to recognize, for a given passage, the organization and the creation and preservation of coherence, for example:

- "Which of the following transitional phases would increase coherence if added to the beginning of sentence 3 ?"

- "Which of the following would make the best concluding sentence to the paragraph above?"

▶ Some questions will test your understanding of organizational and presentation strategies in print, electronic, and visual media, for example:

- "The information in which of the following paragraphs in the passage would be best represented by a graphical chart?"

- "Which of the following types of chart would best represent the information in sentence 2 of the excerpt?"

★ Make sure you are familiar with the following major organizational patterns for texts:

— Compare and contrast
— Chronological sequence
— Spatial sequence
— Cause and effect
— Problem and solution

★ Make sure you are familiar with the following types of graphs and charts, the differences between them, and the appropriateness of each for presenting different types of information:

— Bar graph
— Line graph
— Pie chart

★ For each print or nonprint medium below, think about the typical organizational patterns used and why each is appropriate:

— Textbooks
— Journal articles
— Newspaper articles
— Television news programs

▶ Some questions will test your ability to recognize different discourse aims and the key features of the major types of discourse, for example:

• "Which of the following evaluative criteria is most appropriate to apply when evaluating a persuasive essay?"

• "Which of the following strategies is most prevalent in the passage?"

• "Which of the following techniques is found in creative discourse more frequently than in expository discourse?"

★ List the key aims and features of

— Creative discourse
— Expository discourse
— Persuasive discourse

▶ Some questions will test your ability to recognize methods of argument and types of appeals in a given passage, for example:

• "Which of the following strategies is used in the passage?"

• "An advertising endorsement by an experienced software developer for a new technological product is an example of ..."

★ Be able to describe each of these elements as a rhetorical strategy and make up some examples of each:

— Use of an analogy or extended metaphor
— Appeal to authority
— Appeal to emotion

▶ Some questions will test your ability to recognize, for a given passage, elements of style, tone, voice, and point of view as part of rhetorical strategy, including sarcasm, criticism, and praise, for example,

• "Which of the following best describes the tone of the passage?"

• "The style of the passage suggests that the writer believes ..."

▶ Some questions will ask you to recognize bias, stereotypes, inferences, and assumptions or will ask you to distinguish between fact and opinion, for example:

• "The phrase in quotation marks in the passage works persuasively because it refers to ..."

• "Which of the following student responses is based on a stereotype?"

Chapter 4

Don't Be Defeated by Multiple-Choice Questions

▶ ▶ ▶ ▶ ▶ ▶ ▶ ▶ ▶ ▶ ▶ ▶

Why the Multiple-Choice Tests Take Time

When you take the practice questions, you will see that there are very few simple identification questions of the "Which of the following authors wrote *Moby Dick*?" sort. When The Praxis Series™ Assessments were first being developed by teachers and teacher educators across the country, it was almost universally agreed that prospective teachers should be able to analyze situations, synthesize material, and apply knowledge to specific examples. In short, they should be able to think as well as to recall specific facts, figures, or formulas. Consequently, you will find that you are being asked to think and to solve problems on your test. Such activity takes more time than simply answering identification questions.

In addition, questions that require you to analyze situations, synthesize material, and apply knowledge are usually longer than are simple identification questions. The Praxis Series test questions often present you with something to read (a case study, a sample of student work, a chart or graph) and ask you questions based on your reading. Strong reading skills are required, and you must read carefully. Both on this test and as a teacher, you will need to process and use what you read efficiently.

If you know your reading skills are not strong, you may want to take a reading course. College campuses have reading labs that can help you strengthen your reading skills.

Understanding Multiple-Choice Questions

You will probably notice that the word order in multiple-choice questions (or syntax) is different from the word order you're used to seeing in ordinary things you read, like newspapers or textbooks. One of the reasons for this difference is that many such questions contain the phrase "which of the following."

The purpose of the phrase "which of the following" is to limit your choice of answers only to the list given. For example, look at this question.

Which of the following is a flavor made from beans?

(A) Strawberry

(B) Cherry

(C) Vanilla

(D) Mint

You may know that chocolate and coffee are flavors made from beans also. But they are not listed, and the question asks you to select from among the list that follows ("which of the following"). So the answer has to be the only bean-derived flavor in the list: vanilla.

Notice that the answer can be submitted for the phrase "which of the following." In the question above, you could insert "vanilla" for "which of the following" and have the sentence "Vanilla is a flavor made from beans." Sometimes it helps to cross out "which of the following" and insert the various choices. You may want to give this technique a try as you answer various multiple-choice questions in the practice test.

Also, looking carefully at the "which of the following" phrase helps you to focus on what the question is asking you to find and on the answer choices. In the simple example above, all of the answer choices are flavors. Your job is to decide which of the flavors is the one made from beans.

The vanilla bean question is pretty straightforward. But the phrase "which of the following" can also be found in more challenging questions. Look at this question:

Entries in outlines are generally arranged according to which of the following relationships of ideas?

(A) Literal and inferential

(B) Concrete and abstract

(C) Linear and recursive

(D) Main and subordinate

The placement of "which of the following" tells you that the list of choices is a list of "relationships of ideas." What are you supposed to find as an answer? You are supposed to find the choice that describes how entries, or ideas, in outlines are related.

Sometimes it helps to put the question in your own words. Here, you could paraphrase the question as "How are outlines usually organized?" Since the ideas in outlines usually appear as main ideas and subordinate ideas, the answer is (D).

TIP Don't be put off by words you don't understand. It might be easy to be upset by words like "recursive" or "inferential." Read carefully to understand the question and look for an answer that fits. An outline is something you are probably familiar with and expect to teach to your students. So slow down, and use what you know. Don't make the questions more difficult than they are. Don't read for "hidden meanings" or "tricks." There are no "trick questions" on The Praxis Series Subject Assessments. They are intended to be serious, straightforward tests of subject knowledge.

You may find that it helps you to circle or underline each of the critical details of the question in your test book so that you don't miss any of them. It's only by looking at all parts of the question carefully that you will have all of the information you need to answer the question.

Circle or underline the critical parts of what is being asked in this question.

> According to research, effective vocabulary instruction integrates new information with familiar information. Which of the following approaches would best provide such integration?
>
> (A) Dictionary reference
>
> (B) Structural cues
>
> (C) Anticipation guide
>
> (D) Semantic feature analysis

Here is one possible way you may have annotated the question:

> According to research, effective <u>vocabulary instruction</u> integrates new information with familiar information. Which of the following <u>approaches</u> would best provide such integration?
>
> (A) Dictionary reference
>
> (B) Structural cues
>
> (C) Anticipation guide
>
> (D) Semantic feature analysis

After spending a minute with the question, you can probably see that you are being asked to recognize the approach that helps students organize their knowledge and integrate new words and concepts into these knowledge structures. (The answer is (D), because semantic feature analysis is an instructional practice that uses a reader's prior knowledge. It shows students how words that are closely related contain some similar characteristics and some different characteristics.)

The important thing is understanding what the question is asking. With enough practice, you should be able to determine what any question is asking. Knowing the answer is, of course, a different matter, but you have to understand a question before you can answer it.

It takes more work to understand "which of the following" questions when there are even more words in a question. Questions that require application or interpretation invariably require extra reading.

Consider this question.

> A famous athlete is eating a large bowl of her favorite cereal. She relates how good and nutritious the cereal is for maintaining good health. Everyone should eat a bowlful each morning for breakfast.
>
> The statement above illustrates which of the following types of persuasive appeal?
>
> (A) Snobbery
>
> (B) Plain folks
>
> (C) Bandwagon
>
> (D) Testimonial

Given the placement of the phrase "which of the following," you can tell that the list of answer choices is a list of "persuasive appeal" techniques. You are supposed to pick the technique that is illustrated by the statement.

Being able to select the right answer depends on your understanding of the statement given. The athlete presents herself as an example of someone whose health and fitness have been enhanced by eating the cereal; she attests to its beneficial effects. The fact that the testimony comes from a famous athlete adds to its persuasiveness. She is perceived as both an authority on and an example of good health, and her statement suggests that eating the cereal can help others become more like her. The correct answer is (D).

Understanding Questions Containing "NOT," "LEAST," "EXCEPT"

In addition to "which of the following" and details that must be understood, the words "NOT," "EXCEPT," and "LEAST" often make comprehension of test questions more difficult. These words are always capitalized when they appear in The Praxis Series test questions, but they are easily (and frequently) overlooked.

For the following test question, determine what kind of answer you're looking for and what the details of the question are.

Which of the following sentences does NOT contain a malapropism?

(A) All her life she searched for the bluebeard of happiness.

(B) I've always had mixed givings about him.

(C) Laughter is the best anecdote for unhappiness.

(D) The starting pay is low, but workers will have many fringe benefits.

You're looking for the sentence that does NOT contain a malapropism (an error in word choice in which a similar-sounding word or group of words is substituted for the correct form). (D) is the answer — that is, all of the other choices do contain a malapropism. (In (A), "bluebeard" should be "bluebird"; in (B), "mixed givings" should be "misgivings"; and in (C), "anecdote" should be "antidote.")

TIP It's easy to get confused while you're processing the information to answer a question with a LEAST, NOT, or EXCEPT in the question. If you treat the word "LEAST," "NOT," or "EXCEPT" as one of the details you must satisfy, you have a better chance of understanding what the question is asking. And when you check your answer, make "LEAST," "NOT," or "EXCEPT" one of the details you check for.

Understanding Questions Based on Reading Passages

Questions based on passages of fiction, nonfiction, and poetry require a careful strategy that balances time, efficiency, and critical understanding.

Since the literature passages can often be dense and complex, you should read through the excerpt before reading the questions, but you should not spend time taking notes or reading the excerpt multiple times until you know what the questions are asking you to do.

For example, you might encounter a poetic excerpt like this:

> If the rude throng pour with furious pace,
> And hap to break thee from a friend's embrace,
> Stop short; nor struggle through the crowd in vain,
> But watch with careful eye the passing train.

(This is from John Gay's *Trivia*, Book III.)

You might be asked a question about the rhyme scheme, or about the meaning of a word, or about the syntax. It makes sense to read the four lines through once to get a basic understanding, then read the question, then go back to the poem to analyze the aspect that will lead you to answering the question.

The strategy of reading the passage through once at a fairly quick pace is especially important for longer passages. Consider the passage below, taken from the novel *The Blood of the Lamb* by Peter De Vries.

> "It's your silly theologies that have made religion impossible and mucked up people's lives till you can't call it living any more! Look at Ma! Look at Pa!"
>
> *Line*　　Look at them indeed. Our mother was wiping the
> (5)　table with one hand and her eyes with the other. Our father had his elbows on the table and seemed to be trying to extricate his head from his hands as from a porthole, or vise, into which it had been inadvertently thrust. My uncle put his face up close to Louie's and
> (10)　said, "You're talking to a servant of God!"
>
> "You're talking to someone who hasn't let the brains God gave him rot, and doesn't intend to!"
>
> Such a scene may seem, to households devoid of polemic excitement, to lie outside credulity, but it was
> (15)　a common one in ours. Now when I am myself no longer assailed by doubts, being rather lashed by certainties, I can look back on it with a perspective quite lacking in my view of it then, for my teeth were chattering.

Once you have gained an overall understanding from reading the passage through once, you can go back to the appropriate section to answer the first question:

> Lines 5-9 depict the father's reaction to the argument as one of
>
> (A)　self-absorption and disinterest
>
> (B)　slow-growing fury with his family
>
> (C)　unshakable support for his son Louie
>
> (D)　distress and helplessness

For the second and third questions, you may need to read the entire passage again, with careful attention to the major influences on the household and the narrator's own stance vis-à-vis the family situation.

> The glimpse the reader receives of the narrator's household reveals most clearly
>
> (A)　the influence of religious zeal on family relations
>
> (B)　the intellectual value of sharing ideas freely in a family
>
> (C)　the effect of culture on relations between younger and older people
>
> (D)　religious fervor in a household unaccustomed to it

In reflecting on the family situation he has described, the narrator does which of the following?

(A) Explains his inability to adopt a point of view different from that of his parents.

(B) Reveals that his family's good-natured polemics gave him confidence.

(C) Contrasts his present state of mind with his former fear as an immediate observer.

(D) Admits that emotion prevents him from being objective.

(The answers to these three questions are (D), (A), and (C), respectively.)

Be Familiar with Multiple-Choice Question Types

Now that you have reviewed the basics of succeeding at multiple-choice questions, it should help to review the most common question formats you are likely to see.

1. Complete the statement

In this type of question, you are given an incomplete statement. You must select the choice that will make the completed statement correct.

In a holistic evaluation of student essays, evaluations are made on the basis of the

(A) number and variety of errors made by each student

(B) overall quality of each student's essay in relation to the topic

(C) ability of each student to communicate in a variety of discourse modes

(D) maturity of the student's handwriting and level of diction

To check your answer, reread the question and add your answer choice at the end. Be sure that your choice best completes the sentence. (The correct answer is (B).)

2. Which of the Following

This question type is discussed in detail in a previous section. The question contains the details that must be satisfied for a correct answer, and it uses "which of the following" to limit the choices to the four choices shown, as this example demonstrates.

> Which of the following groups contains three words that are pronounced differently depending on whether they are used as nouns or verbs?
>
> (A) lick, bottle, can
>
> (B) table, herd, carpet
>
> (C) drive, catalog, board
>
> (D) sow, entrance, present

(The correct answer is (D).)

3. Roman numeral choices

This format is used when there can be more than one correct answer in the list. Consider the following example.

> Of the sentences below, which two contain a weak reference?
>
> I. The principal disapproved of the students' wearing shorts in school.
>
> II. We spent the whole day on a bird-watching expedition, but we didn't see one.
>
> III. Joe found time for his composing whenever he could, but none of his music was ever published.
>
> IV. He was an excellent horseman, but he never owned any.
>
> (A) I and III
>
> (B) I and IV
>
> (C) II and III
>
> (D) II and IV

One useful strategy in this type of question is to assess each possible answer before looking at the answer choices, then evaluate the answer choices. In the question above, sentence II and sentence IV contain weak references (a "weak reference" is a grammatical term that describes a situation in which a pronoun used in a sentence is not clearly linked to the noun to which the pronoun is supposed to refer). So the correct answer is (D).

4. Questions containing LEAST, EXCEPT, NOT

This question type is discussed at length above. It asks you to select the choice that doesn't fit. You must be very careful with this question type, because it's easy to forget that you're selecting the negative. This question type is used in situations in which there are several good solutions, or ways to approach something, but also a clearly wrong way to do something.

5. Questions with reading passages

This question type is also discussed at length above. Remember to read the passage through first, and then answer the questions, referring back to the passage as necessary.

6. Other Formats

New formats are developed from time to time in order to find new ways of assessing knowledge with multiple-choice questions. If you see a format you are not familiar with, read the directions carefully. Then read and approach the question the way you would any other question, asking yourself what you are supposed to be looking for, and what details are given in the question that help you find the answer.

Useful Facts about the Test

1. **You can answer the questions in any order.** You can go through the questions from beginning to end, as many test takers do, or you can create your own path. Perhaps you will want to answer questions in your strongest field first and then move from your strengths to your weaker areas. There is no right or wrong way. Use the approach that works for you.

2. **There are no trick questions on the test.** You don't have to find any hidden meanings or worry about trick wording. All of the questions on the test ask about subject matter knowledge in a straightforward manner.

3. **Don't worry about answer patterns.** There is one myth that says that answers on multiple-choice tests follow patterns. There is another myth that there will never be more than two questions with the same lettered answer following each other. There is no truth to either of these myths. Select the answer you think is correct, based on your knowledge of the subject.

4. **There is no penalty for guessing.** Your test score is based on the number of correct answers you have, and incorrect answers are not counted against you. When you don't know the answer to a question, try to eliminate any obviously wrong answers and then guess at the correct one.

5. **It's OK to write in your test booklet.** You can work problems right on the pages of the booklet, make notes to yourself, mark questions you want to review later, or write anything at all. Your test booklet will be destroyed after you are finished with it, so use it in any way that is helpful to you.

Smart Tips for Taking the Test

1. **Put your answers in the right "bubbles."** It seems obvious, but be sure that you are "bubbling in" the answer to the right question on your answer sheet. You would be surprised at how many candidates fill in a "bubble" without checking to see that the number matches the question they are answering.

2. Skip the questions you find to be extremely difficult. There are bound to be some questions that you think are hard. Rather than trying to answer these on your first pass through the test, leave them blank and mark them in your test booklet so that you can come back to them. Pay attention to the time as you answer the rest of the questions on the test and try to finish with 10 or 15 minutes remaining so that you can go back over the questions you left blank. Even if you don't know the answer the second time you read the questions, see if you can narrow down the possible answers, and then guess.

3. Keep track of the time. Bring a watch to the test, just in case the clock in the test room is difficult for you to see. Remember that, on average, you have one minute to answer each of the 120 questions. One minute may not seem like much time, but you will be able to answer a number of questions in only a few seconds each. You will probably have plenty of time to answer all of the questions, but if you find yourself becoming bogged down in one section, you might decide to move on and come back to that section later.

4. Read all of the possible answers before selecting one — and then reread the question to be sure the answer you have selected really answers the question being asked. Remember that a question that contains a phrase like "Which of the following does NOT. . ." is asking for the one answer that is NOT a correct statement or conclusion.

5. Check your answers. If you have extra time left over at the end of the test, look over each question and make sure that you have filled in the "bubble" on the answer sheet as you intended. Many candidates make careless mistakes that could have been corrected if they had checked their answers.

6. Don't worry about your score when you are taking the test. No one is expected to get all of the questions correct. Your score on this test is not analogous to your score on the SAT, the GRE, or other similar tests. It doesn't matter on this test whether you score very high or barely pass. If you meet the minimum passing scores for your state, and you meet the other requirements of the state for obtaining a teaching license, you will receive a license. Your actual score doesn't matter, as long as it is above the minimum required score. With your score report you will receive a booklet entitled *Understanding Your Praxis Scores*, which lists the passing scores for your state.

Chapter 5
Practice Questions

Practice Questions

Now that you have studied the content topics and have worked through strategies relating to multiple-choice questions, you should take the following practice test. You will probably find it helpful to simulate actual testing conditions, giving yourself about 90 minutes to work on the questions. You can cut out and use the answer sheet provided if you wish.

Keep in mind that the test you take at an actual administration will have different questions, although the proportion of questions in each area and major subarea will be approximately the same. You should not expect the percentage of questions you answer correctly in these practice questions to be exactly the same as when you take the test at an actual administration, since numerous factors affect a person's performance in any given testing situation.

When you have finished the practice questions, you can score your answers and read the explanations of the best answer choices in chapter 6.

THE PRAXIS

S E R I E S

Professional Assessments for Beginning Teachers®

TEST NAME:
English Language, Literature, and Composition: Content Knowledge

Practice Questions

Time—90 Minutes
90 Questions

(Note, at the official test administration, there will be 120 questions, and you will be allowed 120 minutes to complete the test.)

DO NOT USE INK

Use only a pencil with soft black lead (No. 2 or HB) to complete this answer sheet.
Be sure to fill in completely the oval that corresponds to the proper letter or number.
Completely erase any errors or stray marks.

PRAXIS
SERIES
Professional Assessments for Beginning Teachers®

Answer Sheet C

PAGE 1

1. NAME

Enter your last name and first initial.
Omit spaces, hyphens, apostrophes, etc.

Last Name (first 6 letters)   F I

(A–Z ovals grid)

2.

YOUR NAME:
(Print)

Last Name (Family or Surname)   First Name (Given)   M. I.

MAILING ADDRESS:
(Print)

P.O. Box or Street Address   Apt. # (If any)

City   State or Province

Country   Zip or Postal Code

TELEPHONE NUMBER: ( )   ( )
Home   Business

SIGNATURE: **TEST DATE:**

3. DATE OF BIRTH

Month	Day
Jan.	
Feb.	
Mar.	
April	
May	
June	
July	
Aug.	
Sept.	
Oct.	
Nov.	
Dec.	

4. SOCIAL SECURITY NUMBER

(0–9 ovals grid)

5. CANDIDATE ID NUMBER

(0–9 ovals grid)

6. TEST CENTER / REPORTING LOCATION

Center Number   Room Number

Center Name

City   State or Province

Country

7. TEST CODE / FORM CODE

(0–9 ovals grid)

8. TEST BOOK SERIAL NUMBER

9. TEST FORM

10. TEST NAME

Educational Testing Service, ETS, the ETS logo, and THE PRAXIS SERIES:PROFESSIONAL ASSESSMENTS FOR BEGINNING TEACHERS and its logo are registered trademarks of Educational Testing Service.

ETS Educational Testing Service

51055 • 08920 • TF71M500   Q2573-06
MH01159

I.N. 202974   1 2 3 4

PAGE 2

CERTIFICATION STATEMENT: (Please write the following statement below. DO NOT PRINT.)
"I hereby agree to the conditions set forth in the *Registration Bulletin* and certify that I am the person whose name and address appear on this answer sheet."

_____

_____

_____

SIGNATURE: _____ DATE: _____ / _____ / _____
                                                    Month   Day   Year

BE SURE EACH MARK IS DARK AND COMPLETELY FILLS THE INTENDED SPACE AS ILLUSTRATED HERE: ● .

1 Ⓐ Ⓑ Ⓒ Ⓓ   41 Ⓐ Ⓑ Ⓒ Ⓓ   81 Ⓐ Ⓑ Ⓒ Ⓓ   121 Ⓐ Ⓑ Ⓒ Ⓓ
2 Ⓐ Ⓑ Ⓒ Ⓓ   42 Ⓐ Ⓑ Ⓒ Ⓓ   82 Ⓐ Ⓑ Ⓒ Ⓓ   122 Ⓐ Ⓑ Ⓒ Ⓓ
3 Ⓐ Ⓑ Ⓒ Ⓓ   43 Ⓐ Ⓑ Ⓒ Ⓓ   83 Ⓐ Ⓑ Ⓒ Ⓓ   123 Ⓐ Ⓑ Ⓒ Ⓓ
4 Ⓐ Ⓑ Ⓒ Ⓓ   44 Ⓐ Ⓑ Ⓒ Ⓓ   84 Ⓐ Ⓑ Ⓒ Ⓓ   124 Ⓐ Ⓑ Ⓒ Ⓓ
5 Ⓐ Ⓑ Ⓒ Ⓓ   45 Ⓐ Ⓑ Ⓒ Ⓓ   85 Ⓐ Ⓑ Ⓒ Ⓓ   125 Ⓐ Ⓑ Ⓒ Ⓓ
6 Ⓐ Ⓑ Ⓒ Ⓓ   46 Ⓐ Ⓑ Ⓒ Ⓓ   86 Ⓐ Ⓑ Ⓒ Ⓓ   126 Ⓐ Ⓑ Ⓒ Ⓓ
7 Ⓐ Ⓑ Ⓒ Ⓓ   47 Ⓐ Ⓑ Ⓒ Ⓓ   87 Ⓐ Ⓑ Ⓒ Ⓓ   127 Ⓐ Ⓑ Ⓒ Ⓓ
8 Ⓐ Ⓑ Ⓒ Ⓓ   48 Ⓐ Ⓑ Ⓒ Ⓓ   88 Ⓐ Ⓑ Ⓒ Ⓓ   128 Ⓐ Ⓑ Ⓒ Ⓓ
9 Ⓐ Ⓑ Ⓒ Ⓓ   49 Ⓐ Ⓑ Ⓒ Ⓓ   89 Ⓐ Ⓑ Ⓒ Ⓓ   129 Ⓐ Ⓑ Ⓒ Ⓓ
10 Ⓐ Ⓑ Ⓒ Ⓓ   50 Ⓐ Ⓑ Ⓒ Ⓓ   90 Ⓐ Ⓑ Ⓒ Ⓓ   130 Ⓐ Ⓑ Ⓒ Ⓓ
11 Ⓐ Ⓑ Ⓒ Ⓓ   51 Ⓐ Ⓑ Ⓒ Ⓓ   91 Ⓐ Ⓑ Ⓒ Ⓓ   131 Ⓐ Ⓑ Ⓒ Ⓓ
12 Ⓐ Ⓑ Ⓒ Ⓓ   52 Ⓐ Ⓑ Ⓒ Ⓓ   92 Ⓐ Ⓑ Ⓒ Ⓓ   132 Ⓐ Ⓑ Ⓒ Ⓓ
13 Ⓐ Ⓑ Ⓒ Ⓓ   53 Ⓐ Ⓑ Ⓒ Ⓓ   93 Ⓐ Ⓑ Ⓒ Ⓓ   133 Ⓐ Ⓑ Ⓒ Ⓓ
14 Ⓐ Ⓑ Ⓒ Ⓓ   54 Ⓐ Ⓑ Ⓒ Ⓓ   94 Ⓐ Ⓑ Ⓒ Ⓓ   134 Ⓐ Ⓑ Ⓒ Ⓓ
15 Ⓐ Ⓑ Ⓒ Ⓓ   55 Ⓐ Ⓑ Ⓒ Ⓓ   95 Ⓐ Ⓑ Ⓒ Ⓓ   135 Ⓐ Ⓑ Ⓒ Ⓓ
16 Ⓐ Ⓑ Ⓒ Ⓓ   56 Ⓐ Ⓑ Ⓒ Ⓓ   96 Ⓐ Ⓑ Ⓒ Ⓓ   136 Ⓐ Ⓑ Ⓒ Ⓓ
17 Ⓐ Ⓑ Ⓒ Ⓓ   57 Ⓐ Ⓑ Ⓒ Ⓓ   97 Ⓐ Ⓑ Ⓒ Ⓓ   137 Ⓐ Ⓑ Ⓒ Ⓓ
18 Ⓐ Ⓑ Ⓒ Ⓓ   58 Ⓐ Ⓑ Ⓒ Ⓓ   98 Ⓐ Ⓑ Ⓒ Ⓓ   138 Ⓐ Ⓑ Ⓒ Ⓓ
19 Ⓐ Ⓑ Ⓒ Ⓓ   59 Ⓐ Ⓑ Ⓒ Ⓓ   99 Ⓐ Ⓑ Ⓒ Ⓓ   139 Ⓐ Ⓑ Ⓒ Ⓓ
20 Ⓐ Ⓑ Ⓒ Ⓓ   60 Ⓐ Ⓑ Ⓒ Ⓓ   100 Ⓐ Ⓑ Ⓒ Ⓓ   140 Ⓐ Ⓑ Ⓒ Ⓓ
21 Ⓐ Ⓑ Ⓒ Ⓓ   61 Ⓐ Ⓑ Ⓒ Ⓓ   101 Ⓐ Ⓑ Ⓒ Ⓓ   141 Ⓐ Ⓑ Ⓒ Ⓓ
22 Ⓐ Ⓑ Ⓒ Ⓓ   62 Ⓐ Ⓑ Ⓒ Ⓓ   102 Ⓐ Ⓑ Ⓒ Ⓓ   142 Ⓐ Ⓑ Ⓒ Ⓓ
23 Ⓐ Ⓑ Ⓒ Ⓓ   63 Ⓐ Ⓑ Ⓒ Ⓓ   103 Ⓐ Ⓑ Ⓒ Ⓓ   143 Ⓐ Ⓑ Ⓒ Ⓓ
24 Ⓐ Ⓑ Ⓒ Ⓓ   64 Ⓐ Ⓑ Ⓒ Ⓓ   104 Ⓐ Ⓑ Ⓒ Ⓓ   144 Ⓐ Ⓑ Ⓒ Ⓓ
25 Ⓐ Ⓑ Ⓒ Ⓓ   65 Ⓐ Ⓑ Ⓒ Ⓓ   105 Ⓐ Ⓑ Ⓒ Ⓓ   145 Ⓐ Ⓑ Ⓒ Ⓓ
26 Ⓐ Ⓑ Ⓒ Ⓓ   66 Ⓐ Ⓑ Ⓒ Ⓓ   106 Ⓐ Ⓑ Ⓒ Ⓓ   146 Ⓐ Ⓑ Ⓒ Ⓓ
27 Ⓐ Ⓑ Ⓒ Ⓓ   67 Ⓐ Ⓑ Ⓒ Ⓓ   107 Ⓐ Ⓑ Ⓒ Ⓓ   147 Ⓐ Ⓑ Ⓒ Ⓓ
28 Ⓐ Ⓑ Ⓒ Ⓓ   68 Ⓐ Ⓑ Ⓒ Ⓓ   108 Ⓐ Ⓑ Ⓒ Ⓓ   148 Ⓐ Ⓑ Ⓒ Ⓓ
29 Ⓐ Ⓑ Ⓒ Ⓓ   69 Ⓐ Ⓑ Ⓒ Ⓓ   109 Ⓐ Ⓑ Ⓒ Ⓓ   149 Ⓐ Ⓑ Ⓒ Ⓓ
30 Ⓐ Ⓑ Ⓒ Ⓓ   70 Ⓐ Ⓑ Ⓒ Ⓓ   110 Ⓐ Ⓑ Ⓒ Ⓓ   150 Ⓐ Ⓑ Ⓒ Ⓓ
31 Ⓐ Ⓑ Ⓒ Ⓓ   71 Ⓐ Ⓑ Ⓒ Ⓓ   111 Ⓐ Ⓑ Ⓒ Ⓓ   151 Ⓐ Ⓑ Ⓒ Ⓓ
32 Ⓐ Ⓑ Ⓒ Ⓓ   72 Ⓐ Ⓑ Ⓒ Ⓓ   112 Ⓐ Ⓑ Ⓒ Ⓓ   152 Ⓐ Ⓑ Ⓒ Ⓓ
33 Ⓐ Ⓑ Ⓒ Ⓓ   73 Ⓐ Ⓑ Ⓒ Ⓓ   113 Ⓐ Ⓑ Ⓒ Ⓓ   153 Ⓐ Ⓑ Ⓒ Ⓓ
34 Ⓐ Ⓑ Ⓒ Ⓓ   74 Ⓐ Ⓑ Ⓒ Ⓓ   114 Ⓐ Ⓑ Ⓒ Ⓓ   154 Ⓐ Ⓑ Ⓒ Ⓓ
35 Ⓐ Ⓑ Ⓒ Ⓓ   75 Ⓐ Ⓑ Ⓒ Ⓓ   115 Ⓐ Ⓑ Ⓒ Ⓓ   155 Ⓐ Ⓑ Ⓒ Ⓓ
36 Ⓐ Ⓑ Ⓒ Ⓓ   76 Ⓐ Ⓑ Ⓒ Ⓓ   116 Ⓐ Ⓑ Ⓒ Ⓓ   156 Ⓐ Ⓑ Ⓒ Ⓓ
37 Ⓐ Ⓑ Ⓒ Ⓓ   77 Ⓐ Ⓑ Ⓒ Ⓓ   117 Ⓐ Ⓑ Ⓒ Ⓓ   157 Ⓐ Ⓑ Ⓒ Ⓓ
38 Ⓐ Ⓑ Ⓒ Ⓓ   78 Ⓐ Ⓑ Ⓒ Ⓓ   118 Ⓐ Ⓑ Ⓒ Ⓓ   158 Ⓐ Ⓑ Ⓒ Ⓓ
39 Ⓐ Ⓑ Ⓒ Ⓓ   79 Ⓐ Ⓑ Ⓒ Ⓓ   119 Ⓐ Ⓑ Ⓒ Ⓓ   159 Ⓐ Ⓑ Ⓒ Ⓓ
40 Ⓐ Ⓑ Ⓒ Ⓓ   80 Ⓐ Ⓑ Ⓒ Ⓓ   120 Ⓐ Ⓑ Ⓒ Ⓓ   160 Ⓐ Ⓑ Ⓒ Ⓓ

FOR ETS USE ONLY | R1 | R2 | R3 | R4 | R5 | R6 | R7 | R8 | TR | CS

ENGLISH LANGUAGE, LITERATURE, AND COMPOSITION: CONTENT KNOWLEDGE

"Death, death, O amiable lovely death."
"Parting is such sweet sorrow."

1. Which of the following is present in both of these lines from Shakespeare's *Romeo and Juliet*?

   (A) Personification
   (B) Oxymoron
   (C) Simile
   (D) Conceit

Questions 2-5 are based on the following excerpt from Amy Lowell's poem "Fireworks."

       You hate me and I hate you.
       And we are so polite, we two!

       But whenever I see you, I burst apart
Line   And scatter the sky with my blazing heart.
 (5)   It spits and sparkles in stars and balls,
       Buds into roses — and flares, and falls.

       Scarlet buttons, and pale green disks,
       Silver spirals and asterisks,
       Shoot and tremble in a mist
(10)   Peppered with mauve and amethyst.

       I shine in the windows and light up the trees,
       And all because I hate you, if you please.

       And when you meet me, you rend asunder
       And go up in a flaming wonder
(15)   Of saffron cubes, and crimson moons,
       And wheels all amaranths and maroons.

          from *The Complete Poetical
          Works of Amy Lowell,* by
          Amy Lowell. Copyright © 1955 by
          Houghton Mifflin Co., Copyright ©
          1983 by Houghton Mifflin Co. Reprinted
          and made available by permission of the
          Trustees under the Will of Amy Lowell.

2. In the excerpt, "scatter the sky" (line 4), "spits and sparkles" (line 5), and "flares, and falls" (line 6) are all examples of

   (A) onomatopoeia
   (B) assonance
   (C) internal rhyme
   (D) alliteration

3. In line 13, "rend asunder" creates an image of

   (A) tearing apart
   (B) overheating
   (C) becoming angry
   (D) becoming lost

4. Which of the following literary elements is most prevalent throughout the excerpt?

   (A) Personification
   (B) Metaphor
   (C) Foreshadowing
   (D) Allusion

5. It can be inferred from the poem that the speaker

   (A) is incapable of love
   (B) is an artist
   (C) enjoys the conflict described
   (D) dislikes fireworks

Questions 6-8 are based on the following excerpt from Charles Dickens' *Great Expectations*.

My sister, Mrs. Joe Gargery, was more than twenty years older than I, and had established a great reputation with herself and her neighbours because she had brought me up "by hand." Having at that time to find out for myself what the expression meant, and knowing her to have a hard and heavy hand, and to be much in the habit of laying it upon her husband as well as upon me, I supposed that Joe Gargery and I were both brought up by hand.

She was not a good-looking woman, my sister, and I had a general impression that she must have made Joe Gargery marry her by hand. Joe was a fair man, with curls of flaxen hair on each side of his smooth face, and with eyes of such a very undecided blue that they seemed to have somehow got mixed with their own whites. He was a mild, good-natured, sweet-tempered, easy-going, foolish, dear fellow—a sort of Hercules in strength and also in weakness.

6. The point of view in the passage is

   (A) first person
   (B) second person
   (C) third person, limited
   (D) third person, omniscient

7. In the passage, the character of Mrs. Gargery is developed primarily through the author's depiction of her

   (A) effect on other people
   (B) most prominent physical traits
   (C) husband's opinion of her
   (D) reputation among her neighbors

8. Which of the following is used in the description of Joe Gargery in the second paragraph?

   (A) Allusion
   (B) Simile
   (C) Metonymy
   (D) Irony

Questions 9-10 are based on the following choices.

   (A) The human race is said to be growing taller, but our stomachs are evidently shrinking. In the past when oysters were eaten at all, a serving of only six or a dozen would have been considered ridiculously small.
   (B) Although oysters have fluctuated in popularity as food, people seem to have been eating them from the time people first appeared.
   (C) If you could bring together the shells of all the oysters consumed by humans since we have been around, they would stack up to mountains that would reach to the stars.
   (D) Oyster eating was a worldwide phenomenon before the Phoenicians and the Vikings. Apparently people took to it independently on all the temperate-zone coasts of the world where oysters of any sort were available.

9. Which statement uses a metaphor to describe appetite?

10. Which statement contains an example of hyperbole?

Questions 11-12 are based on the following excerpt from Joyce Cary's *The Horse's Mouth*.

I was walking by the Thames. Half-past morning on an autumn day. Sun in a mist. Like an orange in a fried-fish shop. All bright below. Low tide, dusty water and a crooked bar of straw, chicken-boxes, dirt and oil from mud to mud. Like a viper swimming in skim milk. The old serpent, symbol of nature and love.

11. Which of the following best describes the descriptive strategy used most consistently in the excerpt above?

    (A) Fragments connecting a series of perceptions and reactions
    (B) Fragments connecting a series of actions and events
    (C) Fragments connected by water imagery
    (D) Fragments connected by color imagery

12. Which of the following best characterizes the language used to describe the Thames?

    (A) It contains concrete and abstract terms in equal proportions.
    (B) It moves from the local and vernacular to the mythic.
    (C) It consistently employs similes and metaphors instead of factual, declarative statements.
    (D) It is conventional and clichéd.

Questions 13-15 are based on the following excerpt from Shakespeare's *King Richard II*.

O, who can hold a fire in his hand
By thinking on the frosty Caucasus?
Or cloy the hungry edge of appetite
Line By bare imagination of a feast?
(5) Or wallow naked in December snow
By thinking on fantastic summer's heat?
O, no! the apprehension of the good
Gives but the greater feeling to the worse.
Fell sorrow's tooth doth never rankle more
(10) Than when he bites, but lanceth not the sore.

13. In lines 1-6, the speaker makes his point by using

    (A) sentimental appeals
    (B) logical syllogisms
    (C) appeals to authority
    (D) rhetorical questions

14. Lines 1-6 suggest the limitations of which of the following proverbial expressions?

    (A) Out of sight, out of mind
    (B) Haste makes waste
    (C) Beauty is in the eye of the beholder
    (D) Mind over matter

15. Metrical considerations imply that which of the following is to be pronounced as two syllables?

    (A) "fire" (line 1)
    (B) "bare" (line 4)
    (C) "worse" (line 8)
    (D) "sore" (line 10)

Question 16 is based on the following excerpt from Alexander Pope's "Essay on Man."

All nature is but art, unknown to thee;
All chance, direction, which thou canst not see;
All discord, harmony not understood;
All partial evil, universal good;
And spite of pride, in erring reason's spite,
One truth is clear, Whatever is, is right.

16. In line 2, "which thou canst not see" modifies

    (A) "nature" (line 1)
    (B) "art" (line 1)
    (C) "chance" (line 2)
    (D) "direction" (line 2)

Questions 17-18 are based on the following lines from Milton's _Paradise Lost_.

> Him the Almighty Power
> Hurled headlong flaming from the ethereal sky
> With hideous ruin and combustion down
> _Line_ To bottomless perdition, there to dwell
> _(5)_ In adamantine chains and penal fire,
> Who durst defy the Omnipotent to arms.

17. Milton places "Him" first in the sentence to

    (A) be consistent with the typical Elizabethan object-verb pattern
    (B) serve as an appositive to "the Almighty Power"
    (C) focus attention on the character performing the action
    (D) focus attention on the character receiving the action

18. Line 6 modifies

    (A) "Him" (line 1)
    (B) "Almighty Power" (line 1)
    (C) "ethereal sky" (line 2)
    (D) "penal fire" (line 5)

Questions 19-20 are based on the following poem by Robert Herrick.

> Fly me not, though I be gray,
> Lady, this I know you'll say;
> Better look the Roses red,
> _Line_ When with white commingled.
> _(5)_ Black your haires are; mine are white;
> This begets the more delight,
> When things meet most opposite:
> As in Pictures we descry,
> Venus standing Vulcan by.

19. "This" in line 6 refers to

    (A) "the more delight" (line 6)
    (B) "When things meet most opposite" (line 7)
    (C) "Pictures" (line 8)
    (D) "we descry" (line 8)

20. Which of the following statements about the versification of the poem is true?

    (A) The poem is written in blank verse.
    (B) The poem is written in iambic pentameter.
    (C) The poem uses a meter in which each line begins and ends with a stressed syllable.
    (D) The poem uses incremental repetition and sprung rhythm.

21. Which of the following terms best describes a type of fiction that makes use of the grotesque, violent, mysterious, and supernatural?

    (A) Neoclassical
    (B) Gothic
    (C) Modernist
    (D) Absurdist

22. Eugene O'Neill's _Beyond the Horizon_, Tennessee Williams' _The Glass Menagerie_, and Thornton Wilder's _Our Town_ can be placed in which of the following literary categories?

    (A) American drama: 1900–1950
    (B) American novels: 1850–1900
    (C) English novels: 1900–1950
    (D) English comedies: 1850–1900

23. For all of these poets, imagination was a supreme organizing and unifying power; it went beyond merely recording and rearranging sense data to create both itself and the world that an individual could know. To see was to create, by composing exterior experience in accordance with basic principles which rise out of the mind in the process of composition. The way we see is who we are. For them, self-analysis became a prime ingredient of all poetry.

    This passage best describes

    (A) Thomas Hardy, A. E. Housman, and Ezra Pound
    (B) William Wordsworth, Samuel Taylor Coleridge, and Percy Bysshe Shelley
    (C) Alexander Pope, Jonathan Swift, and Samuel Johnson
    (D) Ben Jonson, William Shakespeare, and John Donne

Question 24 is based on the following quatrain, which begins one of Shakespeare's sonnets.

My mistress' eyes are nothing like the sun;
Coral is far more red than her lips' red;
If snow be white, why then her breasts are dun;
If hairs be wires, black wires grow on her head.

24. In these lines, the speaker

    (A) departs from the Renaissance sonnet-writer's stock conventions of praise
    (B) likens the battle of love, through imagery of red and white, to the War of the Roses
    (C) uses traditional Renaissance imagery of color and color contrasts to communicate a new perspective on art
    (D) plays against the rhythms of iambic pentameter in each of the four lines

25. The group of poets most closely associated with the Harlem Renaissance includes

    (A) Countee Cullen, Claude McKay, and Langston Hughes
    (B) Robert Lowell, Sylvia Plath, and Anne Sexton
    (C) Allen Ginsberg, Gregory Corso, and Lawrence Ferlinghetti
    (D) Ishmael Reed, Gwendolyn Brooks, and Nikki Giovanni

26. Which of the following authors is associated with the Colonial, or Puritan, period of American literature?

    (A) Stephen Crane
    (B) William Cullen Bryant
    (C) Anne Bradstreet
    (D) Louisa May Alcott

27. Each of the following novels is paired with its corresponding author EXCEPT:

    (A) *The Color Purple* – Alice Walker
    (B) *Beloved* – Maya Angelou
    (C) *Their Eyes Were Watching God* – Zora Neale Hurston
    (D) *The Joy Luck Club* – Amy Tan

28. He cannot close his ears to the Old Testament challenge: "Canst thou catch Leviathan with a hook?" Instead he becomes in his alienation, his sultanism, his pride, blasphemy, and diabolism more monstrous than the beast he hunts. When on the last day they confront each other, which is the Monster — Leviathan in his "gentle joyousness," his "mighty mildness of repose," or Ahab screaming his mad deviance?

The passage above is from a discussion of a novel by

    (A) Nathaniel Hawthorne
    (B) William Thackeray
    (C) Herman Melville
    (D) Thomas Hardy

Questions 29-31 are based on the excerpts below.

(A)   There lived a wife at Usher's Well,
          And a wealthy wife was she;
      She had three stout and stalwart sons,
          And sent them o'er the sea.

(B)   An Ace of Hearts steps forth: the King unseen
      Lurked in her hand, and mourned his captive
              Queen:
      He springs to vengeance with an eager pace,
      And falls like thunder on the prostrate Ace.
      The nymph exulting fills with shouts the sky;
      The walls, the woods, and long canals reply.

(C)   Who would have thought my shriveled heart
      Could have recovered greenness? It was gone
              Quite underground; as flowers depart
      To see their mother-root, when they have blown,
              Were they together
              All the hard weather,
      Dead to the world, keep house unknown.

(D)   She thanked men, — good! but thanked
      Somehow — I know not how — as if she ranked
      My gift of a nine-hundred-years-old name
      With anybody's gift. Who'd stoop to blame
      This sort of trifling? Even had you skill
      In speech — which I had not — to make your
              will
      Quite clear to such an one, and say, "Just this
      Or that in you disgusts me; here you miss,
      Or there you exceed the mark" — and if she let
      Herself be lessoned so, nor plainly set
      Her wit to yours, forsooth, and made excuse,
      — E'en then would be some stooping; and I
              choose
      Never to stoop.

29. Which is from a mock epic?

30. Which is from a dramatic monologue?

31. Which is an example of the ballad stanza?

Questions 32-33 are based on the following passage.

If you were to go merely by the quantity of his imitators, you could argue that Dashiell Hammett was a more important writer than James Joyce. He gave his imitators more than an attitude; he gave them a cast of characters, a resilient plot, a setting, a repertory of images, a style, a keyhole view of society, an ethos, and, above all, a hero. Sam Spade is an old American type brought up to date, Hawkeye become private eye with fedora and street smarts instead of leather stockings and wood lore, his turf the last frontier of San Francisco.

32. In the last sentence, the comparison of Sam Spade to Hawkeye alludes to novels by

(A) Joseph Conrad
(B) Nathaniel Hawthorne
(C) James Fenimore Cooper
(D) Herman Melville

33. The passage discusses the

(A) shortcomings of authors who lack formal training
(B) value of continuing to teach the classics
(C) characteristics of writers who are essentially derivative and unimaginative
(D) creation of a new popular genre

Questions 34- 37 are based on the poem "Frederick Douglass" by Paul Laurence Dunbar and the student responses below.

A hush is over all the teeming lists,
And there is pause, a breath-space in the strife;
A spirit brave has passed beyond the mists
Line And vapors that obscure the sun of life.
(5) And Ethiopia, with bosom torn,
Laments the passing of her noblest born.
. . . .
For her his voice, a fearless clarion, rung
That broke in warning on the ears of men;
For her the strong bow of his power he strung,
(10) And sent his arrows to the very den
Where grim Oppression held his bloody place
And gloated o'er the mis'ries of a race.
. . . .
Through good and ill report he cleaved his way
Right onward, with his face set toward the heights,
(15) Nor feared to face the foeman's dread array, —
The lash of scorn, the sting of petty spites.
He dared the lightning in the lightning's trace,
And answered thunder with his thunder back.

Student Responses

(A) Student A: This poem is about war. It's about "strife" or "bloody" fighting. The champion "cleaved his way Right onward."

(B) Student B: A famous leader is praised for all the contributions he made to his people. He met much oppression in his struggle for his people but overcame it all.

(C) Student C: This lady, Ethiopia, is very sad when someone close to her dies. This person, who was killed in war, helped people. He must have been some kind of a super warrior or maybe even a god.

(D) Student D: It interested me the way this poem is so concerned with sound and noise. It begins on a quiet note and death but then builds up to the final stanza which is full of sound words and action.

34. Which student response points out the author's appeal to the senses to complement the content of the poem?

35. Which student response provides the best summary of the poem?

36. "What often misleads less able students when they read poetry is the very commonness of some words. Most will look up words they have never seen before; what deceives them are words that they 'know' perfectly well, but 'know' in an inappropriate sense."

In which of the following lines from Dunbar's poem is the underlined word likely to present the kind of problem discussed above?

(A) A hush is over all the teeming <u>lists</u> (line 1)
(B) And there is a pause, a breath-space in the <u>strife</u> (line 2)
(C) A <u>spirit</u> brave has passed beyond the mists (line 3)
(D) And vapors that <u>obscure</u> the sun of life (line 4)

37. To which of the following should a student be referred for the fullest discussion of a word that presents the kind of problem discussed in the previous question?

(A) *The Oxford English Dictionary*
(B) *Baugh's History of the English Language*
(C) *The Random House Dictionary of the English Language*
(D) *Webster's New Collegiate Dictionary*

Questions 38-39 are based on the following excerpt from "The Waltz" by Dorothy Parker.

Why, thank you so much. I'd adore to.

I don't want to dance with him. I don't want to dance with anybody. And even if I did, it wouldn't be him. He'd be well down among the last ten. I've seen the way he dances; it looks like something you do on Saint Walpurgis Night. Just think, not a quarter of an hour ago, here I was sitting, feeling so sorry for the poor girl he was dancing with. And now *I'm* going to be the poor girl. Well, well. Isn't it a small world?

38. After the opening sentence, the excerpt presents an example of an

   (A) omniscient point of view
   (B) unreliable narrator
   (C) interior monologue
   (D) interior dialogue

39. In the final sentence of the excerpt, the question is

   (A) rhetorical
   (B) hypothetical
   (C) leading
   (D) Socratic

Questions 40-44 are based on the following poem, "Root Cellar" by Theodore Roethke.

Nothing would sleep in that cellar, dank as a ditch,
Bulbs broke out of boxes hunting for chinks in the
    dark,
Shoots dangled and drooped,
Line Lolling obscenely from mildewed crates,
(5) Hung down long yellow evil necks, like tropical
    snakes.
And what a congress of stinks!
Roots ripe as old bait,
Pulpy stems, rank, silo-rich,
Leaf-mold, manure, lime, piled against slippery
    planks.
(10) Nothing would give up life:
Even the dirt kept breathing a small breath.

40. In line 1, "sleep" is a metaphorical equivalent for

   (A) die
   (B) darken
   (C) breed
   (D) breathe

41. In context, "that cellar" (line 1) is a place where

   (A) garbage is stored in mildewed crates when ice and snow cover the ground
   (B) household furniture is repaired with the planks kept there
   (C) families store vegetables and canned goods during the summer
   (D) bulbs, roots, and gardening supplies are stored

42. Lines 1-8 describe the effects of the

   (A) force that drives living things to grow
   (B) sterility of the newly scrubbed cellar
   (C) decay that necessarily destroys living things
   (D) disease that afflicts even the plants of a doomed family

43. In the poem, "dank as a ditch" (line 1), "dangled and drooped" (line 3), and "Roots ripe" (line 7) are examples of

   (A) onomatopoeia
   (B) internal rhyme
   (C) alliteration
   (D) assonance

44. Which of the following is the key line that best sums up the major theme of the poem?

   (A) "Bulbs broke out of boxes hunting for chinks in the dark" (line 2)
   (B) "And what a congress of stinks" (line 6)
   (C) "Nothing would give up life" (line 10)
   (D) "Even the dirt kept breathing a small breath" (line 11)

Questions 45-46 are based on two student responses to a writing assignment about "Root Cellar." The assignment was to write a short evaluation of the poem, giving some evidence for the evaluation.

Response I

The poem is very lifelike, picturing accurately the sort of things that are likely to turn up in a cellar. I have seen the kinds of shoots, smelled the stench and manure, and felt the planks the writer talks about. I also think that the theme is accurate: life doesn't give in to death easily. Even the sounds are true to nature. Although I do think some of the sound structures are overdone, I like the natural tones of the poem—there is even something "rooty" in the rhythms. Roethke has a keen eye and a sensitive ear. It's a great poem.

Response II

"Root Cellar" is a poem in which the speaker uses many examples of decaying things that are repugnant to most people—mildewed crates, tropical snakes, congress of stinks, manure, etc. The continued cluster of these pictures makes a strong imagistic whole of the poem. It is even embodied in the title. It's a tight poem; I like it, and we can learn a good deal from it.

45. What is the major critical assumption of the writer of Response I ?

    (A) Poems have subtle themes.
    (B) Realistic writing makes for good poetry.
    (C) Poets express their deeply felt aspirations in poetry.
    (D) Poetry and dreams express people's unconscious desires.

46. What is the major critical assumption of the writer of Response II ?

    (A) It is difficult to readily comprehend a good poem.
    (B) A poem should have a moral.
    (C) Poets should not offend their readers' standards.
    (D) Unified elements make for good poetry.

Questions 47-48 are based on the passage and student responses below. The students were asked to explain the following passage from a Washington Irving story they had recently read.

When Rip Van Winkle returned to his home town after a twenty years' absence, he told the inhabitants that he was "a poor, quiet man, a native of the place, and a loyal subject of the king." They then denounced him as a traitor and a spy.

(A) Student A: This story shows that words and statements can change their meaning because the times change. It was fine to be a loyal subject of the king when Rip Van Winkle left his village, but it was not so fine when he returned. Much of what we say that is acceptable now may not be acceptable in ten years or so.

(B) Student B: Rip Van Winkle doesn't explain why he was away so long, and so the people think that there is something fishy about him. People worried that he wanted to borrow money and they were bothered by his strangeness. They were disturbed by people who are different.

(C) Student C: The point of the story is that people in general are self-concerned and suspicious. They are likely to think the worst of a person and mistrust him from the beginning, maybe because they know that they aren't too trustworthy themselves. It didn't matter what he said.

(D) Student D: The story is very ironic and shows that people are at the mercy of chance or fate. Rip Van Winkle returns home after a long absence and happens to run into the wrong group of people first. They seem to be a left-wing group of terrorists plotting an overthrow. If he had talked to another group first, he probably would have been accepted.

47. Which student has demonstrated the best understanding of this story?

48. Which student appears to have the most cynical view of human nature?

Question 49 is based on the lines below.

> A leaf falls to earth,
> While butterflies float near.
> For each, a mirror.

49. To make this poem fit the structure of a classic haiku, the author should change

    (A) "A leaf" to "Lone leaf"
    (B) "butterflies" to "butterfly"
    (C) "float" to "hover"
    (D) "mirror" to "birth"

Questions 50-51 are based on the following excerpt from D. H. Lawrence's "The Rocking-Horse Winner."

It came whispering from the springs of the still-swaying rocking-horse, and even the horse, bending his wooden, champing head, heard it. The big doll, sitting so pink and smirking in her new pram, could hear it quite plainly, and seemed to be smirking all the more self-consciously because of it. The foolish puppy, too, that took the place of the teddybear, he was looking so extraordinarily foolish for no other reason but that he heard the secret whisper all over the house: "There *must* be more money!"

Yet nobody ever said it aloud. The whisper was everywhere, and therefore no one spoke it. Just as no one ever says: "We are breathing!" in spite of the fact that breath is coming and going all the time.

50. In the passage, the representations of the rocking-horse and doll are examples of

    (A) hyperbole
    (B) metaphor
    (C) allusion
    (D) personification

51. "It" in line 1 refers to which of the following?

    (A) The sound made by the rocking-horse
    (B) An unspoken truth
    (C) The sound of people breathing
    (D) A quantity of hidden money

Question 52 is based on the following excerpt from Shakespeare's *King Lear*.

> See how yond justice rails upon yond simple
>   thief.
> Hark in thine ear. Change places and handy-
>   dandy,
> Which is the justice, which is the thief?
> . . . .
> Through tatter'd clothes small vices do appear.
> Robes and furr'd gown hide all. Plate sin with
>   gold,
> And the strong lance of justice hurtless breaks;
> Arm it in rags, a pygmy's straw does pierce it.

52. Which of the following is the best summary of this passage?

    (A) Everyone deserves a chance to reform.
    (B) Riches and position hide guilt.
    (C) No one can escape retribution.
    (D) Justice is blind.

53. After hearing his students discuss what a tragedy might be, a teacher observes that they have misconceptions that may interfere with their understanding of a tragedy they will be reading. He prepares a list of statements about what constitutes a tragedy, and asks students to indicate whether they agree or disagree with each statement. After reading the play, the class will discuss what their misconceptions were and how they have revised their thinking.

Which of the following comprehension strategies did the teacher use?

    (A) Semantic feature analysis
    (B) Anticipation guide
    (C) Reciprocal teaching
    (D) Background building

54. Aristotle moved from place to place in the Lyceum while he taught. He was the prototype of peripatetic teachers. So say those who enjoyed not only hours, but days, walking with C. S. Lewis or Francis Schaeffer.

    To determine the meaning of the underlined word in the passage above, a student would find which of the following most helpful?

    (A) The use of structural cues
    (B) The use of context cues
    (C) Understanding of figurative language
    (D) Understanding of euphemisms

55. A high school teacher wants to meet the needs of reluctant readers who are required to read Dickens' *Tale of Two Cities*. Which of the following materials is most likely to motivate these students to become engaged in the book?

    (A) A book about Dickens' country and city of origin
    (B) Photographs of the town in which Dickens wrote the novel
    (C) Copies of the novel that are printed in large, easy-to-read print
    (D) Software allowing students to interact with the setting of the novel

56. When the English tongue we speak,
    Why is *break* not rhymed with *freak*?
    Will you tell me why it's true
    We say *sew*, but likewise *few*?
    And the maker of a *verse*
    Cannot cap his *horse* with *worse*.

    The lines above deal with English

    (A) orthography
    (B) metrics
    (C) dialects
    (D) semantics

57. All of the following are pairs of homophones EXCEPT

    (A) paws . . pause
    (B) nun . . none
    (C) gross . . grows
    (D) pedals . . peddles

58. *Simplistic* is often used incorrectly because of its resemblance to the word *simple*. In which of the following sentences is the word *simplistic* used correctly?

    I.   Your *simplistic* ideas sound sensible to me.
    II. Your *simplistic* solutions do not address the difficult situation.
    III. How shall we assess the student's *simplistic* yet heart-felt response to poetry?

    (A) II only
    (B) III only
    (C) I and II
    (D) II and III

59. The epic *Beowulf* and its shorter elegiac contemporaries "The Wanderer" and "The Seafarer" were all originally written in what language?

    (A) Old English
    (B) Middle English
    (C) Elizabethan English
    (D) Early Modern English

60. Which of the following cognates is most different in meaning and usage from its original Latin root?

    (A) Corporate
    (B) Corpulent
    (C) Corpse
    (D) Corporeal

61. "Mary enjoys singing songs, eating spaghetti, and books."

    The sentence above could be improved by

    (A) dividing it into two sentences
    (B) switching "eating spaghetti" with "books"
    (C) adding the word "reading" before "books"
    (D) deleting "eating"

62. Which of the following sentences is grammatically correct?

    (A) It's time for the children to take their nap.
    (B) Jumping off the cliff, the crowd was thrilled by the diver.
    (C) Everybody with tickets are supposed to use the door on the left.
    (D) Please keep this discussion between you and I.

63. Which of the following sentences is correctly punctuated?

    (A) My favorite works of literature are "The Lottery", *The Sun Also Rises*, and "Bartelby the Scrivener."
    (B) My favorite works of literature are "The Lottery", *The Sun Also Rises*, and "Bartelby the Scrivener".
    (C) My favorite works of literature are "The Lottery," *The Sun Also Rises*, and "Bartelby the Scrivener."
    (D) My favorite works of literature are "The Lottery," *The Sun Also Rises*, and "Bartelby the Scrivener".

64. Which of the following lists contains words that are pronounced differently depending on whether they are used as nouns or verbs?

    (A) *paper, supply, chronicle*
    (B) *table, herd, carpet*
    (C) *suspect, conscript, present*
    (D) *drive, catalog, board*

65. Ralph Ellison's *Invisible Man* <u>is</u> a novel about a young African American man's quest for a definable identity. The novel (excluding the Prologue) <u>began</u> in the South. Seven chapters later, the setting <u>will shift</u> to the North, where the protagonist <u>has encountered</u>, among other antagonists, members of the Brotherhood. The novel <u>ends</u> with the protagonist living in a basement apartment while he <u>will be deciding</u> how best to deal with his new identity.

    The paragraph above could best be improved by replacing the underlined words with

    (A) *is; begins; shifts; encounters; ends; decides*
    (B) *is; began; will shift; shall encounter; ended; is deciding*
    (C) *is; has begun; shifts; will encounter; ended; is deciding*
    (D) *was; had begun; has shifted; encounters; will end; decides*

66. The term *regionalism*, once honorably used in the United States to identify the literature of a young and far-flung nation, now too often suggests narrowness and parochialism, a mentality afflicting authors too timid to make it in the big city. Such _____ are, of course, unfair; a novel set in Manhattan's East Side, for example, can be many times more provincial than a tale from the hills or the hollows.

    Which of the following correctly fills the blank?

    (A) connotations
    (B) epigrams
    (C) euphemisms
    (D) denotations

67. *The parking lot is open to members only from 5 A.M. to 7 P.M.*

    Which of the following will resolve the ambiguity of the sentence above?

    (A) Insert the word *always* before *open*.
    (B) Move *only* from after *members* to after *7 P.M.*
    (C) Change *The parking lot is* to *These parking lots are.*
    (D) Change *is open* to *opens.*

Questions 68-69 are based on the following passage.

Any use of language that calls a fire in a nuclear reactor building "rapid oxidation," the illegal overthrow of a legitimate government "destabilizing a government," crimes "inappropriate actions," and lies "inoperative statements" is language that attempts to avoid responsibility, that attempts to make the bad seem good, the negative appear positive, something unpleasant appear attractive, and that seems to communicate but does not. It is language designed to alter our perception of reality and corrupt our minds. Such language does not provide the tools needed to develop and preserve civilization. Such language breeds suspicion, cynicism, distrust, and ultimately, hostility.

68. Which of the following is an example of language use similar to that in the quoted phrases within the passage?

    (A) "Performer" for musician or dancer
    (B) "Let the cat out of the bag" for giving away a secret
    (C) "Opening Pandora's box" for asking a question that raises many problematical issues
    (D) "Rectification of boundaries" for invasion

69. Which of the following statements would best follow the last sentence to complete the passage?

    (A) The effects of such language on a culture, if deleterious, are short-term and minimal.
    (B) However, it does not present a serious problem because it is used and read by only a narrow segment of society.
    (C) It reflects an intellectually appropriate application of ingenuity in treating language as a living and changing organism.
    (D) It is insidious, because it can infect and ultimately destroy the function of language — communication among people and social groups.

70. All of the following statements are basic principles of process writing EXCEPT:

    (A) Students need frequent direct instruction in grammar.
    (B) Students need frequent opportunities to write in class.
    (C) Students need to partner with others to get feedback on their writing.
    (D) Students need to conference with the teacher.

71. Which of the following is LEAST appropriate as a purpose for student journals?

    (A) To provide a place for students to articulate their thoughts about course material
    (B) To serve as a means of evaluating a student's facility with mechanics and rhetorical strategies
    (C) To allow students to practice their writing before handing it in to be graded
    (D) To help students find personal connections to the material they are studying

72. Which of the following activities is generally NOT part of the prewriting stage of the writing process?

    (A) Creating a web
    (B) Creating a Venn diagram
    (C) Composing a formal outline
    (D) Participating in peer review

73. Which of the following is an important principle of process writing?

    (A) It is appropriate for students to eliminate stages in the process as they become practiced writers.
    (B) Some modes of writing are more important than others.
    (C) Students may need to move back and forth through the writing stages.
    (D) The teacher is the best audience for student writing.

        I.   Student self-assessment
       II.   Teacher evaluation of student
       III.   Teacher resource for planning lessons

74. Which of the above are appropriate functions of the writing portfolio?

    (A) I and II only
    (B) I and III only
    (C) II and III only
    (D) I, II, and III

75. Students have written a creative response to a story they have read. Which of the following might be an effective strategy for assessing what they have written?

       I.   The teacher asks each student to develop guidelines after completing the assignment and then the teacher assesses each paper based on the guidelines.
       II.   The teacher works together with students ahead of time to develop a scoring guideline so that they know the expectations for the assignment.
       III.   The teacher asks students to read and respond to each others' papers, using a scoring guideline that the teacher developed, distributed, and discussed before the assignment was given.

    (A) II only
    (B) III only
    (C) I and II only
    (D) II and III only

76. Which of the following describes an appropriate peer-review activity?

    (A) Students evaluate each other's written drafts and offer suggestions for revision.
    (B) Students evaluate a classmate's entire writing portfolio and assign a grade.
    (C) Students select a fellow classmate's graded writing assignment and rewrite it.
    (D) Students critique the teacher's model response to the assignment.

77. Which of the following follows the proper MLA format?

   (A) Jones believes that Vivaldi deserves credit for more than just his prolific output (Jones, 157).
   (B) Jones (157) believes that Vivaldi deserves credit for more than just his prolific output.
   (C) Jones believes that Vivaldi deserves credit for more than just his prolific output. (157)
   (D) Jones believes that Vivaldi deserves credit for more than just his prolific output (157).

78. A student searching online for information about a certain eighteenth-century writer is deluged with false hits because there is a famous race-car driver with the same name. The best strategy for the student to improve the search would be to modify the search string by

   (A) adding the word "book"
   (B) including the name of one of the author's books
   (C) excluding hits that contain the word "race-car"
   (D) sorting the references chronologically

Questions 79-81 are based on the following excerpt from an online tutorial about e-commerce.

   So your customers have ordered a lot of your widgets online. Congratulations! But don't start counting your chickens: You still have some work to do before you make those sales. You can't send customers their products until you calculate taxes and shipping. And more importantly, you still need to determine how to process the customers' preferred methods of payment. The key is to figure out the best software solution for your situation.

79. The word in the passage that most clearly indicates the desired audience is

   (A) calculate
   (B) preferred
   (C) customers
   (D) widgets

80. Which of the following does the author do to gain the attention of the reader?

   (A) Uses euphemism.
   (B) Addresses the reader directly.
   (C) Predicts future profits.
   (D) Attacks a popular idea.

81. The excerpt appeals to its target audience by

   (A) comparing the target audience's product to another product
   (B) praising the success of the target audience
   (C) portraying the interests of the target audience's customers in a positive way
   (D) suggesting that the members of the target audience are highly respected in society

Questions 82-83 are based on the following paragraph.

_____.
A wreck might be valuable for itself, of course, rather than for its cargo or the scrap value of its hull and fittings. A ship like the *Mary Rose* is of historical interest, and her salvaging was more in the nature of an archaeological dig that happened not to be performed on dry land. The *Titanic*, too, is now viewed in a similar light, thanks mainly to some very well-orchestrated publicity intended to supplant the ship's poetic and melancholy status with that of a treasure trove of artifacts.

82. Which of the following would make the most appropriate first sentence for the paragraph?

(A) Salvagers do not bother to recover a wreck unless it involves something of great enough value to make the venture worthwhile.

(B) What really grabs people's attention is the prospect of large ships being found and restored to the upper air.

(C) Newspaper editors understand perfectly that treasure and treasure hunts come very high on the list of things that induce their readers to suspend disbelief.

(D) The principles of researching and locating remain common to both shallow and deep-water wrecks, but the techniques are mostly quite different.

83. References to the *Mary Rose* and the *Titanic* in the paragraph provide

(A) supporting details
(B) necessary transitions
(C) a cause-and-effect relationship
(D) appropriate generalizations

Question 84 is based on the following paragraph.

In the saddest prefatory note I know of, Coleridge says that he dreamed a poem four or five times as long as the "Kubla Khan" we now have. Awakening, he hurried to write it down, but managed only fifty-four lines before "he was unfortunately called out by a person on business from Porlock." On regaining his room, he was dismayed to find that, "with the exception of eight or ten scattered lines and images, all the rest had passed away like the images on the surface of a stream into which a stone has been cast, but, alas! without the after restoration of the latter!"

84. How is supporting evidence primarily presented in the passage?

(A) Direct quotation from a primary source
(B) Indirect quotation via a secondary source
(C) Paraphrasing the views of a single person
(D) Summarizing the argument of an authority

Questions 85-86 are based on the following excerpt.

(1) The overwhelming majority of immigrants to America in the nineteenth century settled in the northeastern and north-central states. (2) The impact of their numbers was staggering. (3) In 1890 New York City contained twice as many Irish as Dublin, the same number of Germans as Hamburg, half as many Italians as Naples, and two and one-half times the Jewish population of Warsaw. (4) Many of these recent immigrants had come willingly, while others had been forced out of their home countries by overpopulation, crop failure, famine, violence, or industrial depression.

85. The information in sentence 3 would best be expressed graphically in the form of a

    (A) map
    (B) pie chart
    (C) bar graph
    (D) line graph

86. In which of the following sources would a student be most likely to find further evidence to support the claims made in sentence 4 ?

    (A) Film footage of immigrants arriving in the United States
    (B) Web site search engines
    (C) Early-twentieth-century American novels
    (D) Primary sources, such as journals and letters written by immigrants

87. Which of the following sentences most likely comes from a piece of writing that defends a particular political view?

    (A) "Humans have been exploring space for only a short time, yet the impact on humanity has been vast."
    (B) "A three-hour debate, televised nationwide, would add considerable weight to the issue."
    (C) "The commercial logic behind such deals centers around the need for companies to refine business practices."
    (D) "A strong and capable military is the foundation of the peace we enjoy today."

Question 88 is based on the following passage.

Our watch will adjust the date automatically for the next 50 years, even during leap years. It will stay accurate to within ten seconds a year, no matter how many times you adjust it for time zone changes. And it requires you to replace the battery just once a decade. There's only one conclusion—you should change your thinking about watches.

88. The advertising strategy most present in the passage is

(A) describing the product's elegance and beauty
(B) making an affective appeal to potential buyers
(C) presenting the product's range of special features
(D) comparing the product with that of a competitor

Question 89 is based on the following passage.

Dr. Johnson was observed by a musical friend of his to be extremely inattentive at a concert while a celebrated soloist played virtuosic flurries of notes on his violin. His friend, to induce him to take greater notice of what was going on, told him how extremely difficult it was to follow the performance. "Difficult do you call it, sir?" replied the doctor. "I wish it were impossible."

89. The tone of Johnson's statement suggests that he was

(A) annoyed by the performance of the solo player
(B) irate at the interruption by his friend
(C) discouraged by his friend's inability to understand the music
(D) disheartened by the solo player's egotistical attitude

90. "He was a most disagreeable companion . . . . His conversation was a procession of one."

This comment by Florence Nightingale about an unidentified man shows most clearly that she is

(A) angered by his condescending attitude
(B) intimidated by his temper
(C) dismayed by his appearance
(D) critical of his vanity

Chapter 6

Right Answers and Explanations for the Practice Questions

▶ ▶ ▶ ▶ ▶ ▶ ▶ ▶ ▶ ▶ ▶ ▶

Right Answers and Explanations for the Practice Questions

Now that you have answered all of the practice questions, you can check your work.
Compare your answers with the correct answers in the table below.

Question Number	Correct Answer	Content Category
1	B	Figurative language and literary elements
2	D	Figurative language and literary elements
3	A	Paraphrasing and interpreting
4	B	Figurative language and literary elements
5	C	Paraphrasing and interpreting
6	A	Figurative language and literary elements
7	A	Figurative language and literary elements
8	A	Figurative language and literary elements
9	A	Figurative language and literary elements
10	C	Figurative language and literary elements
11	A	Patterns, structures, forms, and genres
12	B	Patterns, structures, forms, and genres
13	D	Methods of argument and types of appeals
14	D	Paraphrasing and interpreting
15	A	Patterns, structures, forms, and genres
16	D	Paraphrasing and interpreting
17	D	Methods of argument and types of appeals
18	A	Paraphrasing and interpreting
19	B	Paraphrasing and interpreting
20	C	Patterns, structures, forms, and genres
21	B	Patterns, structures, forms, and genres
22	A	Historical and cultural contexts
23	B	Historical and cultural contexts
24	A	Historical and cultural contexts
25	A	Historical and cultural contexts
26	C	Historical and cultural contexts
27	B	Identifying major works and authors
28	C	Identifying major works and authors
29	B	Patterns, structures, forms, and genres
30	D	Patterns, structures, forms, and genres
31	A	Patterns, structures, forms, and genres
32	C	Identifying major works and authors
33	D	Paraphrasing and interpreting
34	D	Figurative language and literary elements
35	B	Text organization and coherence
36	A	Paraphrasing and interpreting
37	A	The history and development of the English language
38	C	Patterns, structures, forms, and genres
39	A	Figurative language and literary elements
40	A	Figurative language and literary elements
41	D	Paraphrasing and interpreting
42	A	Paraphrasing and interpreting
43	C	Figurative language and literary elements
44	C	Paraphrasing and interpreting
45	B	Recognizing bias, stereotypes, inferences, and assumptions

Question Number	Correct Answer	Content Category
46	D	Recognizing bias, stereotypes, inferences, and assumptions
47	A	Paraphrasing and interpreting
48	C	Style, tone, voice, and point of view
49	C	Patterns, structures, forms, and genres
50	D	Figurative language and literary elements
51	B	Paraphrasing and interpreting
52	B	Paraphrasing and interpreting
53	B	The teaching of reading
54	B	The teaching of reading
55	D	The teaching of reading
56	A	Language acquisition and development
57	C	Language acquisition and development
58	D	The history and development of the English language
59	A	The history and development of the English language
60	A	The history and development of the English language
61	C	Grammar
62	A	Grammar
63	C	Grammar
64	C	Grammar
65	A	Grammar
66	A	Semantics
67	B	Semantics
68	D	Semantics
69	D	Text organization and coherence
70	A	Teaching writing
71	B	Teaching writing
72	D	Teaching writing
73	C	Teaching writing
74	D	Assessing student writing
75	D	Assessing student writing
76	A	Assessing student writing
77	D	Research and documentation techniques
78	C	Research and documentation techniques
79	C	Purpose and audience
80	B	Purpose and audience
81	B	Purpose and audience
82	A	Text organization and coherence
83	A	Text organization and coherence
84	A	Text organization and coherence
85	C	Print, electronic, and visual media
86	D	Research and documentation techniques
87	D	Discourse aims
88	C	Discourse aims
89	A	Style, tone, voice, and point of view
90	D	Style, tone, voice, and point of view

Explanations of Right Answers

ENGLISH LANGUAGE

1. This question tests your knowledge of literary techniques. An oxymoron is a locution that produces an effect by a seeming self-contradiction. The paradoxical phrases "amiable lovely death" and "sweet sorrow" result in poignancy, which adds to these lines and to the play as a whole. Therefore, the correct answer is (B).

2. This question asks you to identify examples of a literary element. Alliteration is the use of several nearby words or stressed syllables beginning with the same consonant. Therefore, (D) is the correct answer.

3. This question asks you to interpret the meaning of a poetic text. "Rend" means *to tear apart*. "Asunder" means *in or into pieces*. Therefore, (A) is the correct answer.

4. This question asks you to recognize the use of a particular literary element in poetry. A metaphor is a figure of speech that makes an implied comparison of two things by directly identifying one with the other. The entire excerpt is an extended metaphor comparing the hatred between the two parties to fireworks ("I burst apart" [line 3]; "I shine in the windows" [line 11]; "you rend asunder / And go up in a flaming wonder" [lines 13-14]). Therefore, (B) is the correct answer.

5. This question asks you to interpret the tone of a poetic text. The speaker describes the conflict as exploding fireworks. Fireworks suggest enjoyment or even a kind of celebration. The descriptions of colors, sounds, and shapes are attractive. The speaker's tone is playful in line 2 ("And we are so polite, we two!") and again in line 12 ("And all because I hate you, if you please"). Therefore, (C) is the correct answer.

6. This question tests your knowledge of narrative point of view. The narrator is a character in the work; uses the first person pronoun (I); and limits the narrative to personal experience, conjecture, and opinion. Therefore, he is a first-person narrator and (A) is the correct answer.

7. This question tests your knowledge of techniques of characterization. In this passage the reader learns about Mrs. Gargery mainly in two ways: first, through the naive narrator's conjecture that the phrase "by hand" refers to her habit of clouting the boy and her husband, and, second, through the indications in the second paragraph that her husband has always submitted to her will. Mrs. Gargery herself is described briefly: "She was not a good-looking woman." But in this passage her sharp temper and the intimidating force of her character are communicated by her effect on the narrator and on her husband Joe. The correct answer, therefore, is (A).

8. This question tests your knowledge of literary terms. In the passage's final line, the narrator directly compares Joe to Hercules, the powerful demigod from Greco-Roman mythology, who was also overcome by a determined woman. Thus, (A) is the correct answer.

9. This question tests your ability to recognize a metaphorical comparison. Sentence (A) states that "our stomachs are shrinking," but that statement is not meant to be taken literally. Rather, the author is using "stomachs" as a metaphor for appetite. The correct answer is (A).

10. This question tests your ability to recognize hyperbole, a figure of speech in which exaggeration is used for emphasis or effect. Claiming that a stack of oysters would constitute "mountains that would reach to the stars" is hyperbole. The correct answer, therefore, is (C).

11. This question tests your ability to identify descriptive patterns and structures and their effects. In this passage, which begins the novel, the author presents a series of quick perceptions of and reactions to the River Thames on an autumn morning. Most of the clauses or phrases that end with periods are actually sentence fragments. The sequence of fragments—"Sun in a mist. Like an orange in a fried-fish shop. All bright below," and so on—builds up the total scene. The correct answer, therefore, is (A).

12. This question tests your knowledge of descriptive conventions. The sun on the Thames is first said to be "Like an orange in a fried-fish shop." The luminous orange among the bland color tones of a local fried-fish shop creates a fresh simile, and it anticipates the scene of disorder at low tide: "dusty water and a crooked bar of straw, chicken-boxes, dirt and oil from mud to mud." Then the simile turns mythical, with the river like a viper shining through the mists; finally, the river becomes "The old serpent, symbol of nature and love." The correct answer, therefore, is (B).

13. This question tests your knowledge of rhetorical strategies. The three questions that constitute lines 1-6 are rhetorical in that the speaker asks them not in order to get information but rather in order to express a conviction. In the lines that follow, the speaker implies that the answer to the series of "who" questions in line 1-6 is, in each case, "no one." The correct answer, therefore, is (D).

14. This question tests your ability to interpret Shakespeare's verse. Lines 1-6 challenge the idea that the mind can control the reactions of the senses by imagining conditions that are contrary to fact. The correct answer, therefore, is (D).

15. This question tests your knowledge of poetic meter. The lines are examples of iambic pentameter. An iambic unit, or foot, consists of an unstressed syllable followed by a stressed syllable. A pentameter line consists of five feet; thus, each line of iambic pentameter verse will contain ten syllables. For the first line of the passage to be read with the required ten syllables, the word "fire" must be pronounced as two syllables. The correct answer, therefore, is (A).

16. This question tests your ability to understand the syntax of the poem. In each of the first four lines, something cited in the first part of the line is given an unexpected definition in the second part of the line. Thus, in line 1, "nature" is defined as concealed art; line 2 defines "chance" as concealed direction. The phrase "which thou canst not see" modifies "direction," just as "unknown to thee" modifies "art" in line 1. The correct answer, therefore, is (D).

17. This question tests your ability to interpret a poetic strategy. Sentences in both Elizabethan and modern English most commonly follow a subject-verb-object pattern. Variations of this word order can, by contrast, stand out and command the reader's attention. In Milton's sentence, the character referred to by the objective pronoun "Him" is the object receiving the action performed by the "Almighty Power." Placing the objective pronoun in the initial position in the sentence has the effect of calling attention to the character represented by the pronoun—not only because the usual pattern of English has

been altered, but also because the reader encounters that word before any others. The correct answer, therefore, is (D).

18. This question tests your ability to understand the syntax of the poem. Line 6 modifies "Him" in line 1. "Him" refers to Satan in the Judeo-Christian belief system; it is Satan who challenges the authority of "the Almighty Power", starts a war in heaven (line 6), and is hurled from heaven to hell (lines 1-5). The correct answer is (A).

19. This question tests your ability to interpret the poem. The demonstrative pronoun "This" in line 6 refers to the thing or experience that, according to the poem, "begets the more delight." Since the poem indicates that the experience is the meeting of opposites, the idea expressed in line 7, the correct answer to this question is (B).

20. This question asks you to identify a characteristic of the poem's meter. Each of the lines of the poem begins with a syllable that is stressed in relation to the syllable that immediately follows it, and each line ends with a syllable that is stressed in relation to the syllable that immediately precedes it. The correct answer, therefore, is (C).

21. This question asks you to identify a type of fiction based on its definition. Gothic fiction is the only choice that matches the description in the question. Well-known examples of Gothic fiction include Mary Shelley's *Frankenstein* and Horace Walpole's *The Castle of Otranto*. Therefore, (B) is the correct answer.

22. This question asks you to place well-known literary works within their historical and categorical contexts. All three works are plays by American playwrights, written between 1922 and 1945. Thus, (A) is the correct answer.

23. This question tests your knowledge of the style of a particular school of writers, the Romantic school. Wordsworth's "Lines Composed a Few Miles above Tintern Abbey" and "The Prelude, or Growth of a Poet's Mind," Coleridge's "Frost at Midnight" and "Dejection: an Ode," and Shelly's "Alastor" are all examples of poems in which the self comes under a great scrutiny and imagination is heralded as an organizing and unifying power. The groups of poets listed in choices (A), (C), and (D) were less concerned with direct self-analysis than the Romantics were. The correct answer, therefore, is (B).

24. This question tests your knowledge of the conventions of a style. The conventional Renaissance (or Petrarchan) sonnet writer glorified a fair-skinned woman with red lips, sparkling eyes, white breasts and golden hair. Here, the speaker asserts at the start of the sonnet that his lover has no such beauty or graces. His straightforward announcement of what she *lacks* rather than of what she *has* is unexpected and puts the reader off guard. This unconventional approach leads to a resolution in the final couplet of the sonnet, where the speaker asserts that, even without the conventional marks of "fairness," his love is more beautiful than any woman "belied with false compare." The correct answer, therefore, is (A).

25. This question tests your knowledge of an important literary movement. Countee Cullen, Claude McKay, and Langston Hughes are poets associated with the Harlem Renaissance, an artistic and cultural movement reflecting the experiences of African Americans. The Harlem Renaissance was centered in the Harlem area of New York City during the 1920's, the era in which the poets listed in (A), the correct answer, achieved their first successes.

26. This question asks you to identify an author within a particular literary time period of American literature. William Cullen Bryant, Louisa May Alcott, and Stephen Crane all wrote in the nineteenth century. Only Anne Bradstreet wrote her poems in New England during the mid-seventeenth century, the Colonial, or Puritan, period of American literature. Therefore, (C) is the correct answer.

27. This question asks you to identify the authors of well-known novels. Maya Angelou is well known as the author of *I Know Why the Caged Bird Sings*. The author of *Beloved* is Nobel prizewinner Toni Morrison. Therefore, (B) is the correct answer.

28. This question tests your knowledge of a well-known work and its author. The passage discusses Melville's novel *Moby Dick*, making (C) the correct answer.

29. This question tests your knowledge of literary genres. Mock epics adopt the elevated style of the epic — including such epic conventions as invocations, formal diction, extended similes, lengthy descriptions of battles, and supernatural interventions — to treat trivial subjects. The disjunction between style and subject usually achieves a satirical effect. The lines in (B), from Alexander Pope's mock epic, *The Rape of the Lock*, present a card game as though it were a battle; in winning the game, Pope's heroine Belinda (referred to as a "nymph" in the fifth line) wins a round in the battle of the sexes that is satirized throughout the poem. The correct answer is (B).

30. This question tests your knowledge of literary genres. The lines of a dramatic monologue are spoken by a character whose personality, motives, and circumstances shape the way he or she tells a story and can, in turn, be inferred from the story told. In the lines of choice (D), from the dramatic monologue "My Last Duchess" by Robert Browning, the character of the speaker, the Duke of Ferrara and that of the young woman he describes are revealed through the Duke's words, but not in the way he intends. While the Duke means to cast the Duchess in an unflattering light, he shows her to be generous and unimpressed by mere rank, and himself to be arrogant, egotistical, and ruthless. The correct answer, therefore, is (D).

31. This question tests your knowledge of literary genres. Ballads are anonymous narrative poems; the ballad stanza is a four-line stanza of alternating tetrameter and trimeter lines with a rhyme of abab or, as in (A), from the Middle English ballad "The Wife of Usher's Well," abcb. The correct answer, therefore, is (A).

32. This question tests your ability to recognize names from a well-known author's novels. Both "Hawkeye" and "Leather-Stocking" were nicknames of Natty Bumppo, the pioneer hero of five novels by James Fenimore Cooper (1789-1851), known collectively as the *Leather-Stocking Tales*. The correct answer, therefore, is (C).

33. This question tests your ability to comprehend the main idea of a passage. The passage asserts that Hammett's imitators wrote novels similar to his and to one another's, thereby creating a body of work that constitutes a genre. That Hammett was widely copied — the passage mentions a "quantity of his imitators" — indicates that the genre was also a popular one. The correct answer, therefore, is (D).

34. This question asks you identify the use of a particular descriptive approach. Student D, noting how the poem moves from a "quiet note" to an ending "full of sound words," focuses on the author's appeal to the senses, particularly the sense of hearing. Students A, B, and C are more concerned with the poem's theme or story than with how the poem achieves its effects. The correct answer, therefore, is (D).

35. This question tests your ability to interpret a poem and recognize an appropriate summary. The poem's subject, as indicated by the title, is Frederick Douglass, an escaped slave who spent most of his life fighting for the rights of African Americans and members of other oppressed groups. It is not, however, necessary to be familiar with Douglass' life to interpret and summarize the poem. As Student B notes, the subject is clearly a brave leader and his struggles. The first sentence of Student B's response summarizes the first two stanzas of the poem; the second sentence summarizes the third stanza. The correct answer, therefore, is (B).

36. This question asks you to evaluate the use of words in a poem. The word "lists" is likely to present a problem in comprehension to some students because these students will know the modern meaning of the word, but will not realize that the word also has a less common, older meaning that is, in fact, more appropriate within the context of the poem. The most common meaning of "lists" is "records or registers of names or items," but "lists" also can denote, as here, the grounds or arena used for combat or competition, a meaning dating from medieval times and practices. The correct answer, therefore, is (A).

37. This question tests your knowledge of reference works for English. Of the references listed, *The Oxford English Dictionary* would be the most appropriate for a student to consult. *The Oxford English Dictionary* gives not only the current, common meanings of a word, but also a history of the different ways a word has been used since its recorded entry into the language. A. C. Baugh's *History of the English Language* is unlikely to treat in depth the meanings of individual words from Dunbar's poem. While dictionaries such as *The Random House Dictionary* and *Webster's New Collegiate Dictionary* often present some of the historical background of a word, neither gives as full a treatment as does *The Oxford English Dictionary*. The correct answer, therefore, is (A).

38. This question asks you to apply your knowledge of literary techniques. The reader hears the narrator's thoughts, and nothing else. Therefore, the correct answer is (C).

39. This question asks you to apply your knowledge of literary elements. The question "Isn't it a small world?" actually makes a statement. A rhetorical question is one where an answer is not expected, or for which there is only one answer. Therefore, the correct answer is (A).

40. This question tests your ability to recognize and interpret figurative language. The word "sleep" in line 1 is best read as a metaphorical equivalent for "die." The word "sleep" in line 1 suggests a state of inactivity that resembles death; the phrase "Nothing would sleep" in line 1 is echoed in line 10, a line that also makes more explicit the notion that nothing in the root cellar would die: "Nothing would give up life." The correct answer, therefore, is (A).

41. This question tests your ability to interpret the poem and draw a correct inference. The poem specifically mentions bulbs (line 2), roots (line 7), and gardening supplies such as manure and lime (line 9). It can be inferred from these lines that these articles have been stored in the cellar for some time: line 2 indicates, for example, that the bulbs have been in the cellar long enough to begin to break out of their boxes, looking for "chinks in the dark." The correct answer, therefore, is (D).

42. This question tests your ability to interpret a poem. The objects in the root cellar continue to manifest a will to live; they are not dormant. The bulbs break out of boxes to "hunt," and shoots come forth. Leaf-mold and manure await their use as fertilizer. Such activity and fertility suggest the refusal of these things to submit to inactivity or death. The correct answer, therefore, is (A).

43. This question tests your ability to recognize a literary technique. Alliteration is the use of several nearby words or stressed syllables beginning with the same consonant. In the poem, "dank as a ditch," "dangled and drooped," and "Roots ripe" are examples of alliteration. The correct answer, therefore, is (C).

44. This question tests your ability to interpret the poem and recognize the main theme. The line that best sums up the major theme of the poem is line 10, "Nothing would give up life." The other lines of the poem serve to illustrate the truth of this statement. The correct answer, therefore, is (C).

45. This question tests your ability to recognize a writer's assumption. The writer of Response I praises various elements of the poem for being "lifelike," "accurate," and "true to nature." The poem's realism is the main criterion this writer uses to evaluate its quality. The correct answer, therefore, is (B).

46. This question tests your ability to recognize a writer's assumption. The implicit assumption in this writer's response to "Root Cellar" is that the quality of a poem is determined by the degree of unity it exhibits. The writer notes that the different images employed by the poem all belong to the same class of things—"decaying things that are repugnant to most people"—and cumulatively create a unified artistic effect. Since this writer admires the poem specifically for its tightness, (D) is the correct answer to the question.

47. This question asks you to combine your knowledge of Washington Irving's story and your ability to evaluate responses to the story. When Rip Van Winkle first falls asleep, he lives in what is still a colony of Great Britain. At that time it is neither unusual nor unlawful to be "a loyal subject of the king," King George III. When Rip wakes up from his nap of twenty years, he is unaware of the profound political and social changes brought about by the American Revolution. Rip's once-conventional statement now makes him appear to be an enemy of American democracy. The correct answer is (A).

48. This question asks you to identify a particular point of view. Student C, who maintains that the point of the story is to show that people are typically selfish and suspicious, regardless of circumstances, expresses a more cynical view of human nature than do the other students. The correct answer is (C).

49. This question asks you to apply your knowledge of literary forms. A classic haiku has five syllables in the first line, seven in the second, and five in the third. The second line in this poem is short one syllable. Therefore, the correct answer is (C).

50. This question asks you to apply your knowledge of literary tools available to the writer. Personification is a figure of speech in which human qualities are attributed to an object, an animal, or an idea. That is, "the horse, bending his wooden, champing head, heard it. The big doll, sitting so pink and smirking in her new pram, could hear it quite plainly, and seemed to be smirking all the more self-consciously because of it." Therefore, the correct answer is (D).

51. This question tests your ability to interpret creative prose in which the referent of the pronoun "it" is separated by several sentences from the pronoun itself. The last line of the first paragraph makes clear what the "it" is —what the toys and puppy are "hearing"— that is, "There *must* be more money!" The second paragraph indicates that this shock over the money situation was shared by all, but never spoken aloud. Therefore, (B) is the correct answer.

52. This question tests your ability to interpret the meaning of the dramatic speech. The passage suggests that the poor and powerless have no way of concealing their vices, while the "Robes and furr'd gowns" worn by people of influence, particularly judges and members of the nobility, cover the guilt of the wearers. The shield metaphor in the last three lines conveys a similar meaning: gold, or money, effectively conceals and protects the sinner from the "lance of justice," or the force of law. The correct answer, therefore, is (B).

53. This question tests your knowledge of important techniques for aiding comprehension. An anticipation guide is a series of questions that students are asked to respond to (usually by marking "Agree" or "Disagree") before a particular unit or lesson is begun. After the unit or lesson, the students review their answers to the anticipation guide and reflect on what they know or understand better. The correct answer, therefore, is (B).

54. This question tests your knowledge of strategies for building students' vocabulary. The word peripatetic is not itself, nor is it surrounded by, figurative language or euphemisms. It does not come from a common Latin or Greek root, nor does it use a common prefix or suffix that would lend help from structural cues. The context around the word ("moved from place to place," "walking with C. S. Lewis or Francis Schaeffer") gives enough clues to help a student figure out that the word must mean "walking about." The correct answer, therefore, is (B).

55. This question asks you to identify a frequently effective way to foster appreciation of reading among students in grades 7-12. Choices (A) and (B), historical in nature and noninteractive, would probably not stimulate many students to make the transition from reluctant to interested. A change in format, reflected in (C), would be unlikely to change students' attitudes. Students often become interested in reading a book if they can interact with aspects of the setting of the book—in the case of Dickens, eighteenth-century France and England. The correct answer, therefore, is (D).

56. This question tests your knowledge of orthography and the relationship between spelling and pronunciation. The lines make the point that often the spellings, or orthography, of words in English do not provide consistent guides to pronunciation. Rhymed words share the same last stressed vowel and the same speech sounds following that vowel. But words sharing identical spellings of those elements do not necessarily rhyme, as the examples of "break" and "freak" and "horse" and "worse" demonstrate. Conversely, though one would not expect words spelled with different vowels to rhyme, the pair "verse" and "worse" shows that sometimes they do. The correct answer, therefore, is (A).

57. This question tests your knowledge of homophones, which are an aspect of language acquisition and the relationship between pronunciation and spelling. Homophones are words that are pronounced alike but differ in written from, origin, and meaning. The pair of words in choices (A), (B), and (D) match this description. The words in (C) are not pronounced alike; the hard "ss" at the end of "gross" is pronounced like the "s" in "sing," whereas the soft "s" at the end of "grows" is pronounced like the "z" in "haze." The correct answer, therefore, is (C).

58. This question tests your ability to detect correct and incorrect uses of a word that is often used incorrectly. Simplistic carries a negative connotation, implying a simple-minded or insufficiently complex approach to an issue. The negative connotation is apparent in II and III, while simplistic is misused with a positive connotation in I. Therefore, (D) is the correct answer.

59. The question tests your knowledge of English language history. *Beowulf* and other Anglo-Saxon works were written in Old English, a Germanic language that gave us some of our most basic, everyday words (e.g., "father," "give," and "day"). (A) is therefore the correct answer.

60. This question asks you to recognize the manifestation of etymological development. These cognates share the Latin root *corpus* or body. All of the current uses connote some aspect of physical body except "corporate." This word has come to mean "united or combined into one collective" and has thus evolved to a meaning more different from its root than the three other choices. Therefore, (A) is the best answer.

61. This question asks you to use your knowledge of the elements of grammatical structures. The first two elements ("singing songs," and "eating spaghetti") set up a specific structure. The writer breaks this structure with the last element. The word "books" should also be the object of an "–ing" verb form to make the construction parallel. Therefore, the correct answer is (C).

62. This question requires you to apply your knowledge of grammar. (B) is misconstructed in that the initial phrase illogically modifies "the crowd," subject of a passive construction. In (C) the verb should be "is"—not "are"—to agree with the singular subject "Everybody."

In (D) the object of the preposition "between" should be "you and me." Sentence (A) is grammatically correct, making it the correct answer.

63. This question requires you to apply your knowledge of the rules of punctuation involving quotation marks. Commas and periods always go inside of quotation marks, whether they are part of the quoted title or not. Therefore, the correct answer is (C).

64. This question tests your knowledge of parts of speech and how certain words can function as more than one part of speech, in this case with a different pronunciation accompanying the functional shift. The correct answer is (C).

65. This question tests your knowledge of verb tense. (B), (C), and (D) create a paragraph in which the use of tense is inconsistent. The correct answer is (A), in which all the verb forms appear in the present tense (the appropriate tense for describing literary action).

66. This question tests your knowledge of semantics, specifically the ability to recognize a reference to connotation. The passage states that "narrowness" and "parochialism" are qualities that have become associated with the term "regionalism." Connotations are notions suggested by or associated with a word that go beyond the word's explicit, or denoted meaning. The correct answer, therefore, is (A).

67. This question tests your ability to recognize how meaning is affected by word order. The ambiguity of the original sentence results from the placement of the modifier "only"; a reader cannot tell whether "only" is intended to modify "members" or the phrase "from 5 A.M. to 7 P.M." If "only" refers to "members," the sentence means that nonmembers cannot park in the parking lot between 5 A.M. and 7 P.M., but members can. If "only" refers to the time period between 5 A.M. and 7 P.M., however, the meaning of the sentence is somewhat different: it means that members can park in the lot from 5 A.M. to 7 P.M. but cannot park there at other times. By changing the position of "only" to make clear that it modifies "from 5 A.M. to 7 P.M.," choice (B) resolves the ambiguity of the sentence and is therefore the best answer.

68. This question tests your knowledge of semantics, especially euphemism. The quoted phrases in the passage illustrate the use of language to hide rather than reveal the realities to which it refers. Similarly, the phrase "rectification of boundaries" in (D) fails to capture the hostility and unlawfulness of an invasion. The correct answer, therefore, is (D).

69. This question tests your ability to complete an argument about semantic practices. The statement in (D) brings the paragraph to synthesis and conclusion by delineating the ultimate effect of the degradation of the language described in the previous few sentences. The degradation of language is condemned throughout the paragraph; none of the other choices preserves the unity of logic of the paragraph. The correct answer, therefore, is (D).

70. This question asks you to recognize some basic principles of process writing. While grammar may be addressed in a mini-lesson, frequent direct instruction is not recognized as an essential aspect of writing instruction. Therefore, in this EXCEPT question, (A) is the correct answer.

71. This question tests your knowledge of approaches to teaching writing. By its very nature, a journal is an informal record of thoughts and experiences and is generally kept for private use. The keeping of journals is a way of encouraging students to write, and write often, on a wide variety of matters that concern them. Because of the informal nature of such journals, students may be less likely to observe the formal rules of mechanics or to use rhetorical strategies demanded in more formal writing; therefore, evaluating students in this way would be inappropriate. The correct answer, the LEAST appropriate purpose, is (B).

72. This question asks you to recognize activities associated with a particular stage of the writing process. All of the options except the last one lead to the production of an organizational structure containing references to potential content. Peer review generally takes place after prewriting and drafting. Therefore, (D) is the correct answer to this NOT question.

73. This question asks you to recognize a basic principle of process writing. The stages of the writing process are recursive. After editing, a student may go back to revise a piece even more. Furthermore, the revision may necessitate a prewriting strategy to generate more content. Therefore, (C) is the correct answer.

74. The question tests your understanding of writing evaluation. Portfolios can be used by students to assess their own writing progress. Studying several semester assignments, they can see both helpful and unhelpful writing patterns developing. From there, they can determine what changes will be necessary in their approach to new assignments. The teacher can also use a student's portfolio for the same purpose: to encourage new directions for the student writer to take. Furthermore, the teacher can evaluate how the class is doing as a whole and decide what modifications in the course need to be made to meet student needs more effectively. Therefore, (D) is the correct answer.

75. This question tests your knowledge of appropriate assessment techniques for writing. Students working on any writing assignment do best when they know the expectations and the audience. In choices II and III, students understand the expectations for the assignment — in choice II they have helped develop the assessment criteria before beginning the assignment. In both cases, students have guidance from the teacher that will help them become better assessors of their writing and, in turn, better writers. In choice I, each student is responsible for developing individual guidelines that the teacher uses to evaluate the assignment. While involving students in the development of assessment criteria is often productive (as in choice II), the scenario presented in choice I provides no opportunity for collaboration between student and teacher or among students and would likely result in frustration on the part of both student and teacher. The correct response is (D).

76. The question tests your understanding of writing evaluation. To be a "peer editor" is to study a fellow classmate's writing and to discover how well the writer is achieving his or her goals. Put another way, the job of the peer editor is to offer encouraging comments and constructive criticism to fellow writers so that they may improve upon what they have already started. The correct answer, therefore, is (A).

77. This question asks you to apply your knowledge of documentation techniques. Since the author's name is in the text, it is not used in the reference. The page number follows the information, but comes before the period. Therefore, the correct answer is (D).

78. This question asks you to apply your knowledge of Internet research techniques. Including a common word such as "book" would not eliminate all the false hits, and including a book title might exclude some desired matches. A chronological list would be based on the date of the material, not the date of its topic. The word "race-car" is likely to appear in most documents about the driver and none about the writer. Therefore, the correct answer is (C).

79. This question asks you to identify a word from the passage that best enables you to identify the intended audience. As can be seen from phrases such as "your customers," "make those sales," and "for your situation," the intended audience is people who are engaged in selling goods to customers. Therefore, (C) is the correct answer.

80. This question asks you to identify a technique used by the author to gain the attention of the reader. Throughout the passage the author addresses the reader directly: "your customers," "you still need," and "You can't send." Therefore, (B) is the correct answer.

81. This question asks you to identify how the advertisement appeals to its target audience. The advertisement congratulates the target audience on its orders before proceeding to a warning about collecting payment and calculating net profit. Therefore, (B) is the correct answer.

82. The question asks you to identify the most appropriate topic sentence for the passage. The passage is primarily concerned with discussing the characteristics that make different shipwrecks attractive to salvagers. Option (A) states that salvagers will not recover a wreck unless it is of great enough value to make the venture worthwhile. Therefore, (A) is the answer.

83. This question tests your ability to recognize the function of certain references. Discussions of the two specific ships supply supporting examples for the assertion in the second sentence that "A wreck might be valuable for itself . . ." The correct answer, therefore, is (A).

84. This question asks you to identify how supporting evidence is presented in the passage. The purpose of the passage is to describe an event in Coleridge's life. The key details of the story are provided by direct quotations from the primary source of the anecdote, Coleridge himself. Therefore, (A) is the correct answer.

85. This question asks you to identify the best way of graphically representing specific information. Sentence 3 compares the ethnic populations of New York City to those of major European cities from which the immigrants came. Because it can visually represent the relative size of each group living in New York and in the referenced European city, the information could best be represented as a bar graph. Therefore, (C) is the correct answer.

86. This question tests your knowledge of appropriate research sources for particular goals. Sentence 4 makes a claim about the immigrants' motives for migration. Primary sources would be most likely to reveal the immigrants' motives. The correct answer, therefore, is (D).

87. This question asks you to identify the sentence that is most likely to come from a piece of writing that is designed to express a political view. Of the four topics addressed in the sentences — space exploration, a political debate, business deals, and the military — the final sentence most directly addresses a political view. Therefore, (D) is the correct answer.

88. This question asks you to identify the advertising strategy most present in the passage. Three of the four sentences in the passage itemize the watch's special features. Therefore, (C) is the correct answer.

89. This question asks you to identify what was annoying Dr. Johnson. Johnson's friend comments that the musical performance was "difficult" to follow. He is using "difficult" in one of its senses to mean "hard to understand." Johnson replies by using a different sense of "difficult," meaning "hard to deal with, manage, or overcome." By using this second meaning of "difficult," Johnson is indicating that he is annoyed by the performance itself. Therefore, (A) is the correct answer.

90. This question asks you to identify Florence Nightingale's criticism of an unnamed man. Nightingale states that his conversation was a "procession of one," that is, that he alone was the subject of the conversation. People who talk only about themselves exhibit vanity. Therefore, (D) is the correct answer.

Chapter 7

Are You Ready? Last-Minute Tips

▶ ▶ ▶ ▶ ▶ ▶ ▶ ▶ ▶ ▶ ▶ ▶

Checklist

❑ Do you know the testing requirements for your teaching field in the state(s) where you plan to teach?

❑ Have you followed all of the test registration procedures?

❑ Do you know the topics that will be covered in each test you plan to take?

❑ Have you reviewed any textbooks, class notes, and course readings that relate to the topics covered?

❑ Do you know how long the test will take and the number of questions it contains? Have you considered how you will pace your work?

❑ Are you familiar with the test directions and the types of questions for your test?

❑ Are you familiar with the recommended test-taking strategies and tips?

❑ Have you practiced by working through the practice test questions at a pace similar to that of an actual test?

❑ If constructed-response questions are part of your test, do you understand the scoring criteria for these items?

❑ If you are repeating a test, have you analyzed your previous score report to determine areas where additional study and test preparation could be useful?

The Day of the Test

You should have ended your review a day or two before the actual test date. And many clichés you may have heard about the day of the test are true. You should

- Be well rested

- Take photo identification with you

- Take a supply of well-sharpened #2 pencils (at least three)

- Eat before you take the test

- Be prepared to stand in line to check in or to wait while other test takers are being checked in

You can't control the testing situation, but you can control yourself. Stay calm. The supervisors are well trained and make every effort to provide uniform testing conditions, but don't let it bother you if the test doesn't start exactly on time. You will have the necessary amount of time once it does start.

You can think of preparing for this test as training for an athletic event. Once you've trained, and prepared, and rested, give it everything you've got. Good luck.

Appendix A
Study Plan Sheet

▶ ▶ ▶ ▶ ▶ ▶ ▶ ▶ ▶ ▶ ▶ ▶

Study Plan Sheet

See Chapter 1 for suggestions on using this Study Plan Sheet.

STUDY PLAN						
Content covered on test	How well do I know the content?	What material do I have for studying this content?	What material do I need for studying this content?	Where could I find the materials I need?	Dates planned for study of content	Dates completed

Appendix B

For More Information

▶ ▶ ▶ ▶ ▶ ▶ ▶ ▶ ▶ ▶ ▶ ▶

Educational Testing Service offers additional information to assist you in preparing for The Praxis Series™ Assessments. *Tests at a Glance* booklets and the *Registration Bulletin* are both available without charge (see below to order). You can also obtain more information from our Web site: www.teachingandlearning.org.

General Inquiries

Phone: 800-772-9476 or 609-771-7395 (Monday-Friday, 8:00 A.M. to 7:45 P.M., Eastern time)
Fax: 609-771-7906

Extended Time

If you have a learning disability or if English is not your primary language, you can apply to be given more time to take your test. The *Registration Bulletin* tells you how you can qualify for extended time.

Disability Services

Phone: 866-387-8602 or 609-771-7780
Fax: 609-771-7906
TTY (for deaf or hard-of-hearing callers): 609-771-7714

Mailing Address

ETS- The Praxis Series
P.O. Box 6051
Princeton, NJ 08541-6051

Overnight Delivery Address

ETS- The Praxis Series
Distribution Center
225 Phillips Blvd.
Ewing, NJ 08628

NOTES

NOTES